SERIES EDITOR: JOHN MOORE

ORDER OF BATTLE 6

GETTYSBURG JULY 2 1863

CONFEDERATE: THE ARMY OF NORTHERN VIRGINIA

JAMES ARNOLD and ROBERTA WIENER

First published in Great Britain in 2000 by Osprey Publishing, Elms Court, Chapel Way, Botley, Oxford OX2 9LP United Kingdom

Email: info@ospreypublishing.com

ISBN 1 85532 855 0

Osprey Series Editor: Lee Johnson
Ravelin Series Editor: John Moore
Research Co-ordinator: Diane Moore
Design: Ravelin Limited, Braceborough, Lincolnshire, United Kingdom
Cartography: Chapman Bounford and Associates, London, United Kingdom
Origination by Valhaven Ltd, Isleworth, United Kingdom
Printed in China through Worldprint Ltd

00 01 02 03 04 10 9 8 7 6 5 4 3 2 1

FOR A CATALOGUE OF ALL BOOKS PUBLISHED BY OSPERY MILITARY, AUTOMOTIVE AND AVIATION PLEASE WRITE TO:
The Marketing Manager, Osprey Direct, P.O. Box 140, Wellingborough, Northants, NN8 4ZA United Kingdom
Email: info@ospreydirect.co.uk

The Marketing Manager, Osprey Direct USA, PO Box 130, Sterling Heights, MI 4311-0130, USA
Email: info@ospreydirectusa.com

VISIT OSPREY AT www.ospreypublishing.com

Series style

The style of presentation adopted in the Order of Battle series is designed to provide quickly the maximum information for the reader.

Order of Battle Unit Diagrams – all 'active' units in the ORBAT, that is those present and engaged on the battlefield are drawn in black. Those units not yet arrived or those present on the battlefield but unengaged are 'shadowed'.

Unit Data Panels – similarly, those units which are present and engaged are provided with company details for infantry and cavalry bodies and with details of the pieces for artillery.

Battlefield Maps – units engaged are shown in the respective colours of their armies. Units shown as 'shadowed' are those deployed for battle but not engaged at the time. Dotted arrows depict actual or planned movements before or after the main action covered by the map.

Order of Battle timelines

Battle page timelines – each volume concerns the Order of Battle for the armies involved. Rarely are the forces available to a commander committed into action as per his ORBAT. To help the reader follow the sequence of events, a timeline is provided at the bottom of each 'battle' page. This timeline gives the following information:

The top line bar defines the actual time of the actions being described in that battle section.

The middle line shows the time period covered by the whole day's action.

The bottom line indicates the page numbers of the other, often interlinked, actions covered in this book.

0800 hrs	0900	1000	1100	1200
pp45-47	48-49 & 52-55	50-51		

Key to Military Series symbols

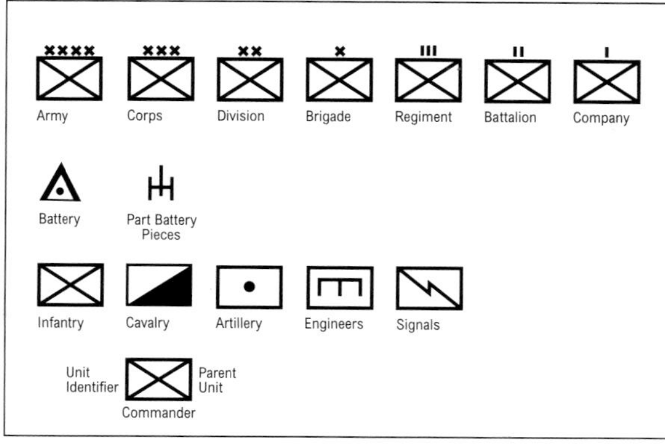

Editor's note

Wherever possible primary sources have been used in compiling the information in this volume.

CONTENTS

THE ARMY OF NORTHERN VIRGINIA

Gettysburg – July 2 1863

Planning

On July 1, at about 1700 hrs, Lieutenant-General James Longstreet had joined General Robert E. Lee on Seminary Ridge. To the east, victorious Confederate soldiers had cleared Gettysburg's streets of the enemy.

But a hostile force of unknown size clung to the high ground south of the town. Longstreet examined the situation for some five to ten minutes. He turned to Lee and strongly urged the army commander to avoid a direct attack against what he judged to be a strong Federal position. Instead, Longstreet recommended that the army move past the Union left and find a position to interpose itself between the yankees and their capital at Washington. This would compel the enemy to attack on ground the Confederates had chosen. This recommendation accorded with Longstreet's predilection for defensive fighting.

Lee responded with the immortal words, 'If the enemy is there tomorrow, we must attack him' and committed his army to an offensive on July 2. Shortly thereafter an aide returned from his reconnaissance of the Federal position. He offered little useful information beyond the obvious: the enemy was present in force. Lee turned to Lieutenant-General Ambrose Hill and Longstreet and said, 'Gentlemen, we will attack the enemy in the morning as early as practicable.'

Lee had not intended to fight a battle so far from base. When the surprise combat at Gettysburg began, he believed that he could not withdraw through Cashtown Gap and still extricate his trains. He could not remain on the defensive because of supply problems. He wrote, 'A battle thus became...unavoidable.'

July 1 ended with the Confederates enjoying a partial success. Heth's and Pender's divisions had met the Union I Corps west of Gettysburg and, after an initial rebuff, driven them through Gettysburg. Providentially, the divisions of Rodes and Early had arrived on the Union flank north of Gettysburg

On the evening of July 1, General Robert Edward Lee made the fateful decision to attack again the next morning. He made his plans in the absence of accurate information about Federal strength. (MARS)

ARMY HEADQUARTERS

Escort/Couriers
39th Battalion Virginia Cavalry
Major John Harvie Richardson

Co. A Captain Augustus Pifer's Co.
Co. C Lee's Body Guard Co. B

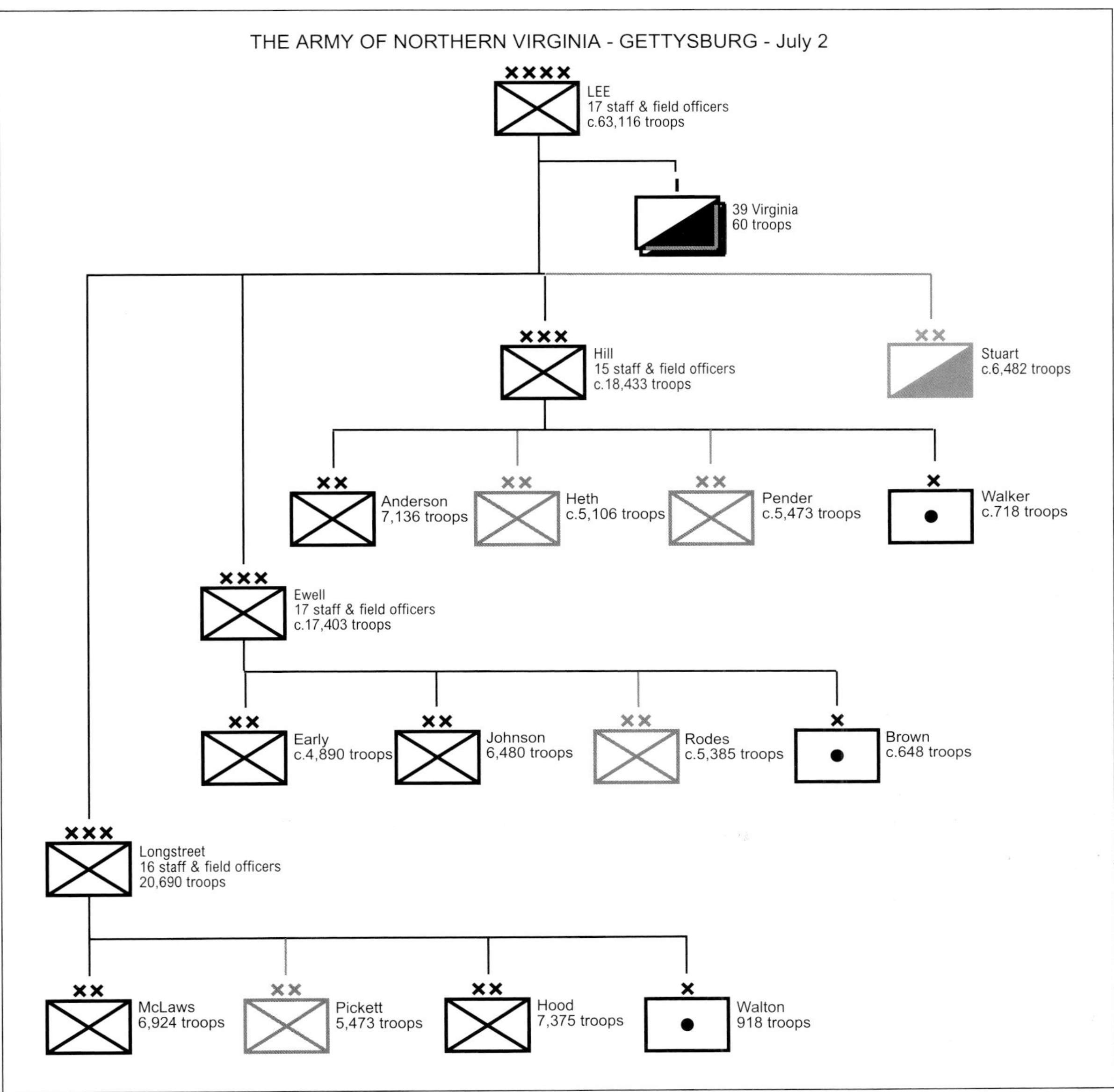

where they routed the Federal XI Corps. Lee was disappointed that more had not been achieved. Reputedly, he told an officer the next day that 'we did not or we could not pursue our advantage of yesterday.'

The Confederates had suffered moderate losses except for Heth's Division. It was so battered that it could not participate in combat the next day. Still, Lee expected to have seven infantry divisions (Pickett's men were still too far distant to figure in the offensive) available for combat on July 2. So far his army had encountered two enemy corps. Because Stuart's cavalry had yet to report, Lee could only guess how many more of the enemy might arrive overnight.

In the absence of accurate intelligence, Lee had to decide where to strike. This was his key decision after his somewhat heated discussion with Longstreet. Lee rode to the Confederate left to confer with the commander of II Corps, Lieutenant-General Richard Ewell. Lee asked Ewell, could his men open the offensive by storming Cemetery Hill at daylight?

Curiously, Major-General Jubal Early replied. Early had visited Gettysburg before the war and claimed a good knowledge of the terrain. He said that an attack from the Confederate left would confront steep, difficult ground. Early recommended turning the enemy's opposite flank via the Round Tops. Ewell and Major-General Rodes approved of Early's statements.

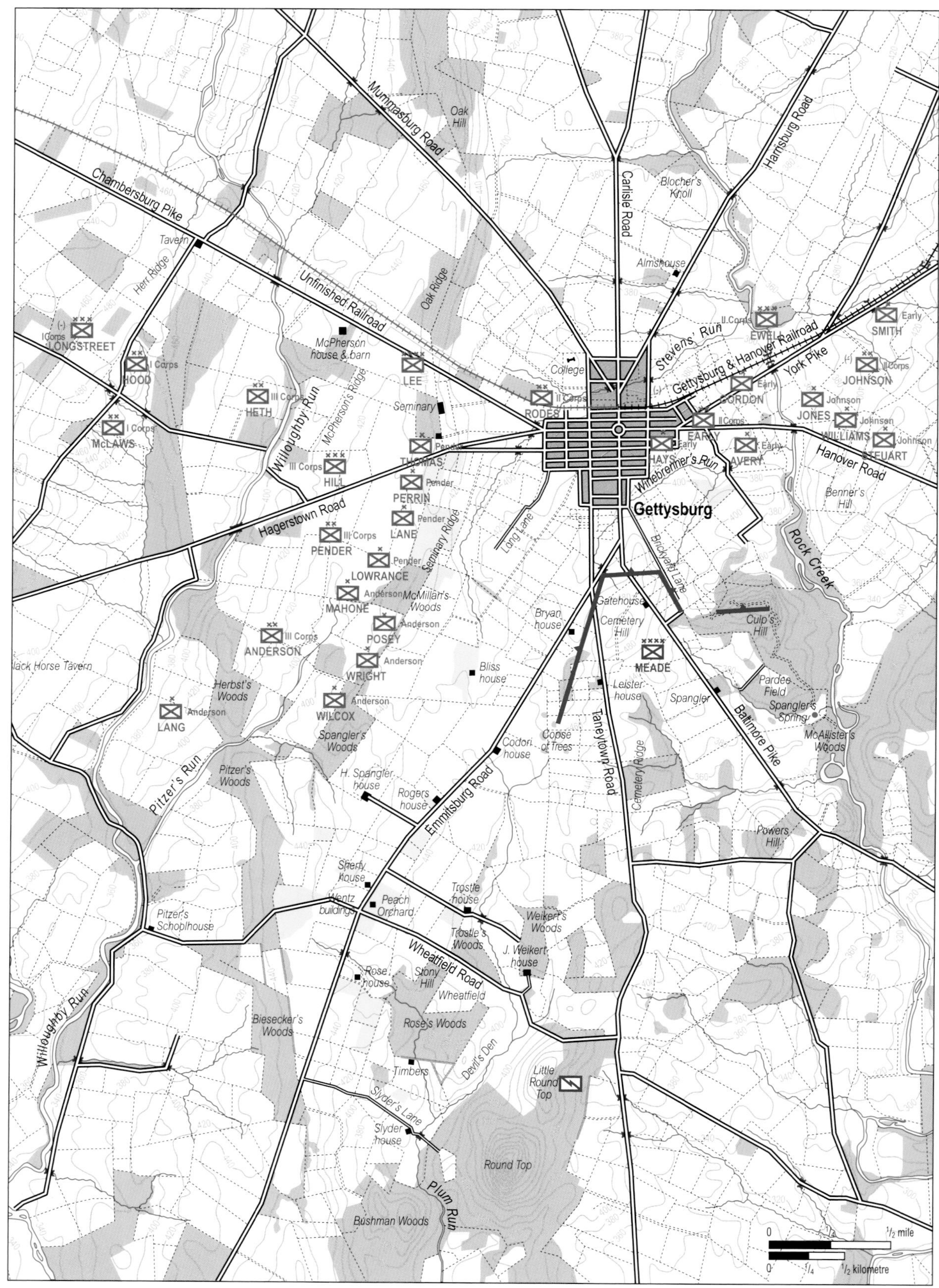

Gettysburg
Mummasburg Road
Oak Hill
Carlisle Road
Harrisburg Road
Blocher's Knoll
Chambersburg Pike
Tavern
Herr Ridge
Unfinished Railroad
Oak Ridge
Almshouse
McPherson house & barn
College
Stevens' Run
Gettysburg & Hanover Railroad
York Pike
Seminary
Willoughby Run
McPherson's Ridge
Hagerstown Road
Seminary Ridge
Long Lane
Winebrenner's Run
Hanover Road
Benner's Hill
Rock Creek
Brickyard Lane
Gatehouse
Cemetery Hill
Culp's Hill
Bryan house
McMillan's Woods
Black Horse Tavern
Herbst's Woods
Bliss house
Leister house
Spangler
Pardee Field
Spangler's Spring
McAllister's Woods
Baltimore Pike
Spangler's Woods
Codori house
Copse of Trees
Taneytown Road
Cemetery Ridge
Pitzer's Run
Pitzer's Woods
H. Spangler house
Rogers house
Emmitsburg Road
Powers Hill
Sherfy house
Wentz buildings
Peach Orchard
Trostle house
Pitzer's Schoolhouse
Weikert's Woods
Trostle's Woods
J. Weikert house
Wheatfield Road
Rose house
Stony Hill
Wheatfield
Biesecker's Woods
Rose's Woods
Devil's Den
Willoughby Run
Timbers
Little Round Top
Slyder's Lane
Slyder house
Round Top
Plum Run
Bushman Woods
LONGSTREET
I Corps
HOOD
McLAWS
HETH
III Corps
HILL
LEE
THOMAS
Pender
PERRIN
LANE
PENDER
LOWRANCE
MAHONE
Anderson
POSEY
ANDERSON
WRIGHT
WILCOX
LANG
RODES
II Corps
EWELL
SMITH
Early
JOHNSON
Johnson
GORDON
JONES
WILLIAMS
STEUART
EARLY
HAYS
AVERY
MEADE
0
1/4
1/2 mile
1/2 kilometre

Lee's dispositions at the start of July 2 and the known Federal positions. The battle dictated that the Army of Northern Virginia operate along exterior lines.

If that were the case, then Lee proposed that II Corps retire from its position in order to close up with the rest of the army. Early again spoke up. It would be detrimental to the soldiers' morale, he said, to cede the ground that they had just won. However, Early promised that II Corps could defend its position.

Lee told the officers that the main attack would occur on the army's opposite flank. The attitude of the II Corps' senior officers disturbed Lee. He returned to his headquarters and decided to order Ewell to withdraw from his position northeast of town.

This order, in turn, clearly upset Ewell. Subsequent to his meeting with Lee, Ewell received reports from scouts that Culp's Hill was undefended. Ewell proposed to capture the heights. Whether Lee believed that Culp's Hill would actually be undefended by the next morning is doubtful. However, Ewell's sudden aggressive spirit restored Lee's faith in his general. He decided to allow II Corps to stay put.

This was a mistake. Lee overlooked the defects in Ewell's position because he thought he could turn the enemy's opposite flank if the remainder of his army applied pressure all along the Union front. He believed Ewell could tie down Union soldiers by attacking from his current position. In fact, Ewell's position was so awkwardly placed that it could neither be reinforced in the event of success nor send reinforcements to support the other corps. According to Colonel Edward Alexander, there was 'no reasonable probability' that Ewell could achieve success against 'almost unassailable' terrain.

Longstreet arose at 0330 hrs on July 2 and arrived at Lee's headquarters by 0500 hrs. He again tried to dissuade Lee from the proposed attack, but Lee was adamant. Lee had already sent one of his staff, Colonel Long, to 'examine and verify' artillery positions to support the attack. Soon after sunrise, Lee ordered his chief of artillery, Brigadier-General Pendleton, to examine the ground along the army's right. Pendleton located a road along Willoughby Run that would serve for the initial phases of the approach march.

In addition, Lee dispatched an engineer officer, Captain Samuel Johnson, to make a thorough reconnaissance. Johnson reported to Lee and Longstreet around 0900 hrs. He confirmed that the Union line stretched south from Cemetery Hill to about only the middle of Cemetery Ridge. Lee asked if Johnson had climbed Little Round Top. Johnson replied yes and that he had seen no enemy troops in that area. Thus the Union flank stood exposed to a Confederate attack. Somehow Johnson had blundered. He had seen no enemy troops at a time when there were numerous Union units present. His incorrect report was to have grave implications for the fate of Longstreet's flank attack.

Lee pitched his headquarters tent near this farm just south of the Chambersburg Pike. Its tenant, a Mrs Thompson, cooked meals for Lee and his staff. (MARS)

Lee rode to Ewell's headquarters. He instructed Ewell to create a diversion when he heard the sound of Longstreet's guns and to make an assault if he thought he could accomplish something useful. Lee returned to Seminary Ridge at about 1000 hrs and testily commented to an aide, 'What can detain Longstreet? He ought to be in position now!'

Longstreet was always careful and meticulous. At Gettysburg, these traits passed beyond the bounds of reason. Because he fundamentally disagreed with Lee's offensive, he failed to show the type of initiative that Lee depended upon.

Around 1100 hrs, Lee sent orders to Longstreet to begin his march to turn the Union left flank. Longstreet requested permission to wait until Law's Brigade arrived. Lee concurred and at least another 40 minutes passed. His original notion to attack in the morning 'as soon as practicable' died stillborn.

As Longstreet departed, Lee's revised plan was to have Longstreet form perpendicular to the Emmitsburg Road on the high ground around the Peach Orchard. From this start line he was to envelop the Union left and drive toward the enemy centre. Hill's corps was to tie down enemy forces opposing it and then advance against the Union centre when Longstreet's flank attack made the situation favourable. Ewell's corps was to make a diversion when Longstreet attacked and make an outright assault if warranted. Major-General Richard Anderson was to have a key role because his division linked Longstreet's efforts with Hill's.

THE ARMY OF NORTHERN VIRGINIA

I CORPS

Lieutenant-General James Longstreet's I Corps was renowned within the Army of Northern Virginia for its tenacious defence and heavy, powerful assaults. It had delivered the knockout punch at Second Manassas, conducted a bloody defensive battle at Sharpsburg, and easily repelled all Union attacks at Fredericksburg. I Corps also enjoyed a command and organisational continuity unlike its two sister corps. The same divisional leaders – McLaws, Hood, and Pickett – had led the same basic units from Fredericksburg on to the invasion of Pennsylvania.

At the corps' helm was the formerly always dependable Longstreet. Officers and men trusted him since they knew that he was unwilling to expose them to unnecessary privation or sacrifice. A British writer described him during the Gettysburg Campaign as a member of 'the class of undemonstrative, unselfish and natural men whose worth is chiefly known to their soldiers.' Indicative of the soldiers' respect for Longstreet was an incident that occurred on July 1. When veterans of the Stonewall Brigade learned that Longstreet was passing nearby, they *ran* to see him. In a newly-organised army that had two officers new to corps command, Lee relied upon the experienced Longstreet, his 'old war-horse', to provide steady leadership.

I CORPS

Lieutenant-General James Longstreet

16 Staff and Field Officers

McLaws' Division
Major-General Lafayette McLaws

Pickett's Division
Major-General George Edward Pickett

Hood's Division
Major-General John Bell Hood/
Brigadier-General Evander McIvor Law

I Corps Reserve Artillery
Colonel James Burdge Walton

Lieutenant-General James Longstreet arrived at Gettysburg ahead of his corps on the evening of July 1 and advised Lee to take up a defensive position between the Federal army and Washington. (U.S. National Archives)

The corps had not participated in the first day of battle around Gettysburg. The end of June 30 had found Hood and McLaws at Greenwood, about 14 miles from Gettysburg. Law's Brigade and Captain William Bachman's German Artillery went to New Guilford to secure the army's flank. Pickett's Division remained outside Chambersburg to guard the army's trains. The men commanded by Hood and McLaws received orders to cook three days' rations early on July 1 in order to be ready for whatever came.

On July 1 McLaws' van division received orders to follow Johnson's II Corps Division on the march to Gettysburg. McLaws dutifully waited alongside the Chambersburg Pike. Trailing close behind Johnson's troops came the II Corps' trains. McLaws asked Longstreet what to do and the corps' commander replied, 'let the trains pass.' It appeared to McLaws that the train was endless. He estimated it was 14 miles long. At 1000 hrs McLaws received another order to wait an hour after the trains passed in order to allow the road to clear and the dust to settle.

Finally, after a ten-hour wait, at 1600 hrs McLaws' Division began its march. Hood's men followed. The divisional artillery accompanied the infantry. The two battalions belonging to the Corps' Artillery Reserve remained in camp. Law's Brigade remained detached.

The start-stop-start march proceeded slowly under

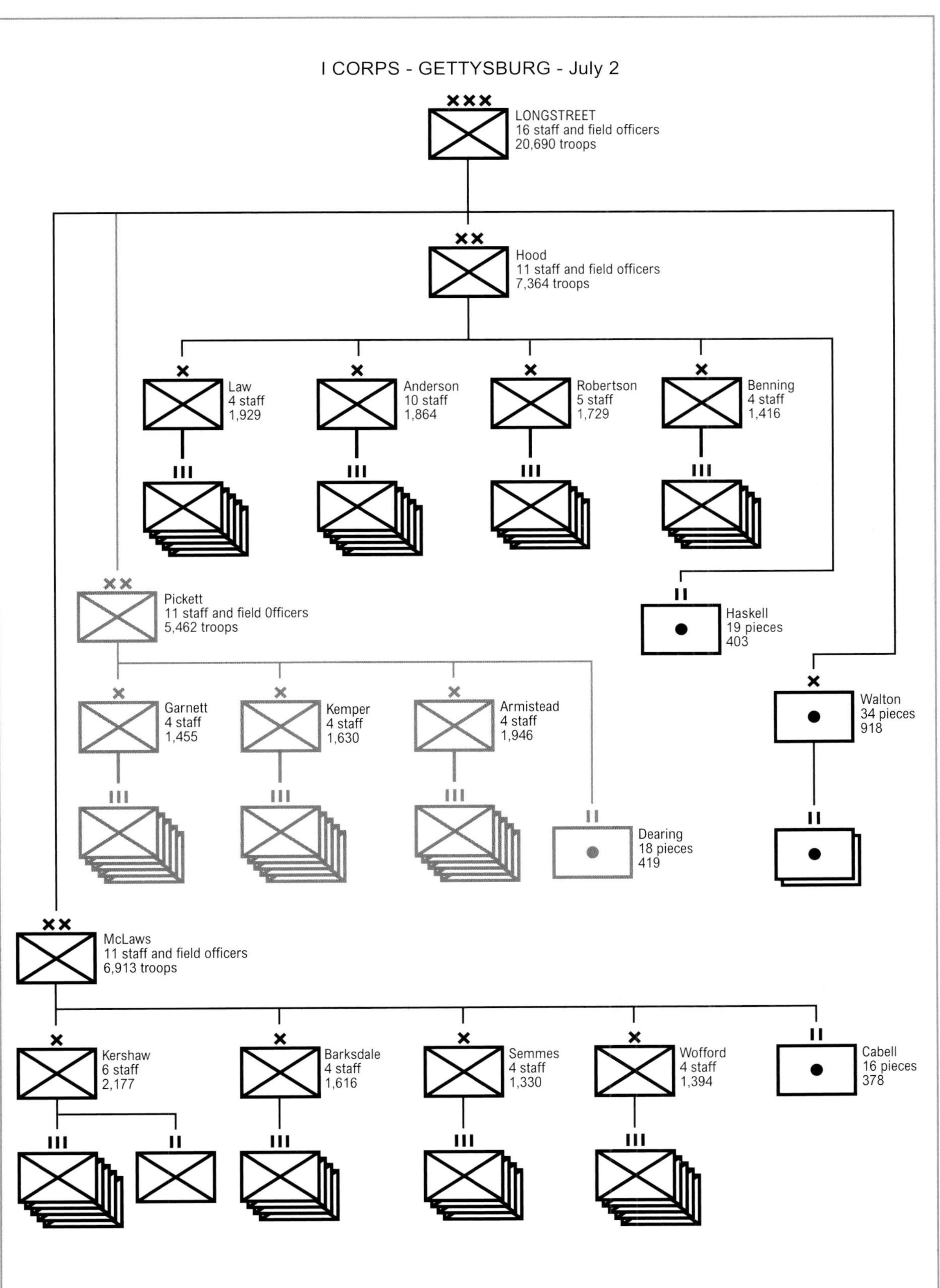
I CORPS - GETTYSBURG - July 2
LONGSTREET
16 staff and field officers
20,690 troops
Hood
11 staff and field officers
7,364 troops
Law
4 staff
1,929
Anderson
10 staff
1,864
Robertson
5 staff
1,729
Benning
4 staff
1,416
Pickett
11 staff and field Officers
5,462 troops
Haskell
19 pieces
403
Garnett
4 staff
1,455
Kemper
4 staff
1,630
Armistead
4 staff
1,946
Walton
34 pieces
918
Dearing
18 pieces
419
McLaws
11 staff and field officers
6,913 troops
Kershaw
6 staff
2,177
Barksdale
4 staff
1,616
Semmes
4 staff
1,330
Wofford
4 staff
1,394
Cabell
16 pieces
378

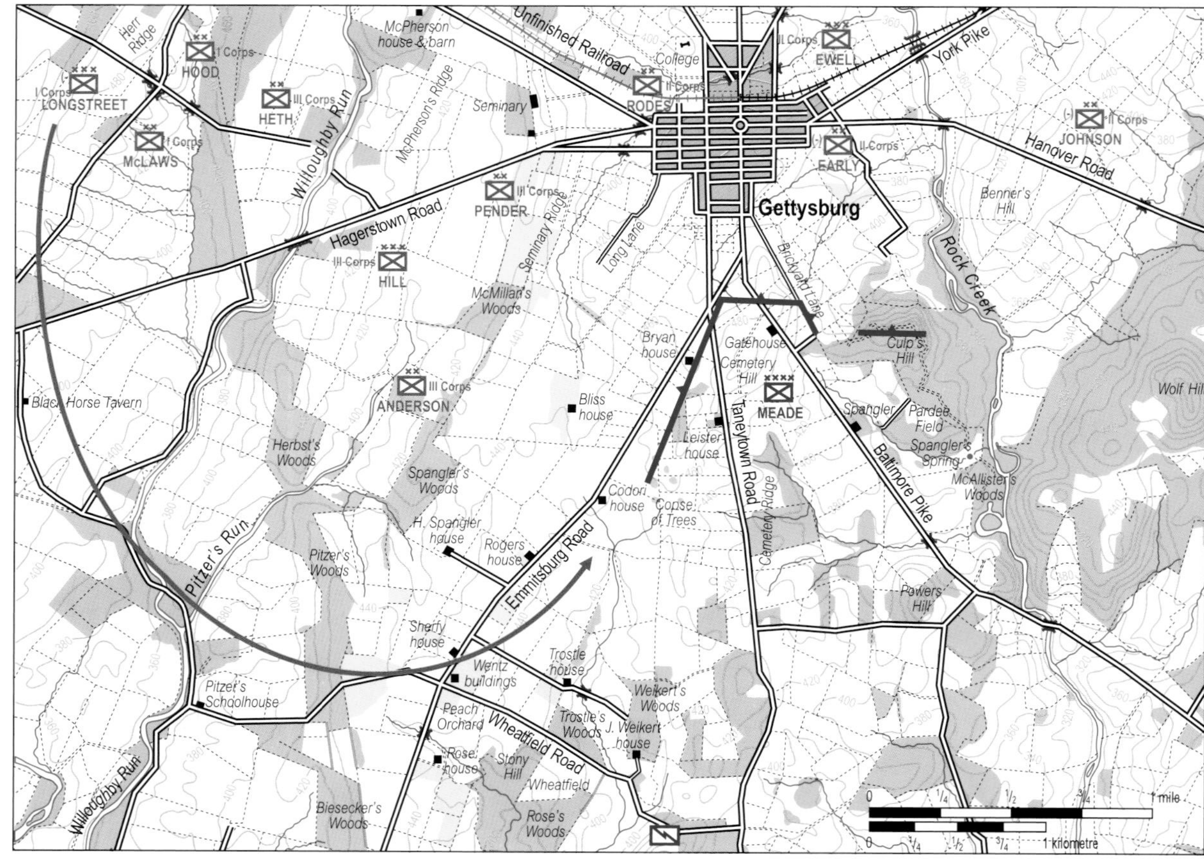

a broiling July sun. When the column reached the top of Cashtown Gap the men heard the sounds of cannon fire around Gettysburg. They cheered and hurried on.

Longstreet returned from a meeting with Lee to find his corps approaching Marsh Creek at around 2200 hrs. He briefed McLaws about what had transpired and ordered him to bivouac at the creek where there was a plentiful supply of water.

McLaws' men went into camp around 2200 hrs. Hood's Division arrived about midnight. It had been a long, tedious day, yet the two divisions had marched for only about 12 miles. Had the army been operating more smoothly, the two divisions with about 12,000 superb veteran soldiers, could easily have reached Gettysburg during daylight and in time to exploit the Confederate successes on July 1.

Additional delays plagued the corps on July 2. McLaws' Division had orders to depart camp at 0400 hrs, yet it did not leave until sunrise. It then waited until around noon before beginning its approach march.

Reputedly, early in the morning, when Hood arrived at Lee's headquarters he found Longstreet and Lee conferring. Lee said to Hood, 'The enemy is here and if we do not whip him, he will whip us.' Then Longstreet took Hood aside and said privately, 'The general is a little nervous this morning. He wishes me to attack. I do not wish to do so without Pickett. I never like to go into battle with one boot off.'

Lee planned for Longstreet's I Corps to make an early, covert march to bring it into position to assault the left flank of the known Federal lines on Cemetery Ridge.

If this account is substantially accurate, then it demonstrates that Longstreet continued to doubt the wisdom of the army's pending offensive. Longstreet's reputation for dependability was to be challenged, because on this field he was to be the officer in charge of the major element of an offensive about which he held grave reservations.

I Corps' Casualties at Gettysburg
July 2, 1863

Infantry killed or wounded 3,634
Infantry missing/captured 576
Artillery killed or wounded 12
Artillery missing/captured 4

I Corps – McLaws' Division

On the afternoon of July 2, Major-General Lafayette McLaws found himself confronting an unsettling view. He had risen early and had his division ready to march by 0400 hrs. For the next eight hours the division essentially marked time while the army's senior leadership decided what to do. McLaws himself had been an unwilling pawn in the struggle between Lee and Longstreet over whether or not the army should assume the offensive and if so, when and how. The incident probably embarrassed and confused McLaws.

The time-consuming counter-march from the Black Horse Tavern area to the division's assigned position on Seminary Ridge did not improve his humour. When the division finally reached its position around 1500 hrs, McLaws saw that he did not face the two regiments and a battery that he had been told to expect. Rather, he saw a powerful Federal force – it was the Union III Corps – deployed on rising ground along a front that stretched beyond McLaws' own right flank.

McLaws notified Longstreet and received the response that 'there was a small force of the enemy in front.' Therefore, Longstreet ordered McLaws to 'proceed at once to the assault.' Realising that instead of conducting a flank-attack against a vulnerable enemy he had to make a frontal attack against an alert and superior force, McLaws deliberately deployed his forces. He later complained to his wife, 'General Longstreet is to blame for not reconnoitering the ground and for persisting in ordering the assault when his errors were discovered.'

McLAWS' DIVISION
Major-General Lafayette McLaws

Kershaw's Brigade - 2,177 troops
Barksdale's Brigade - 1,616 troops
Semmes' Brigade - 1,330 troops
Wofford's Brigade - 1,394 troops
Cabell's Artillery Battalion - 374 troops

On July 2, Major-General Lafayette McLaws had to contend with obstructed marching routes, inadequate reconnaissance, conflicting orders and a strained relationship with his Corps' commander, as well as a determined enemy. (MARS)

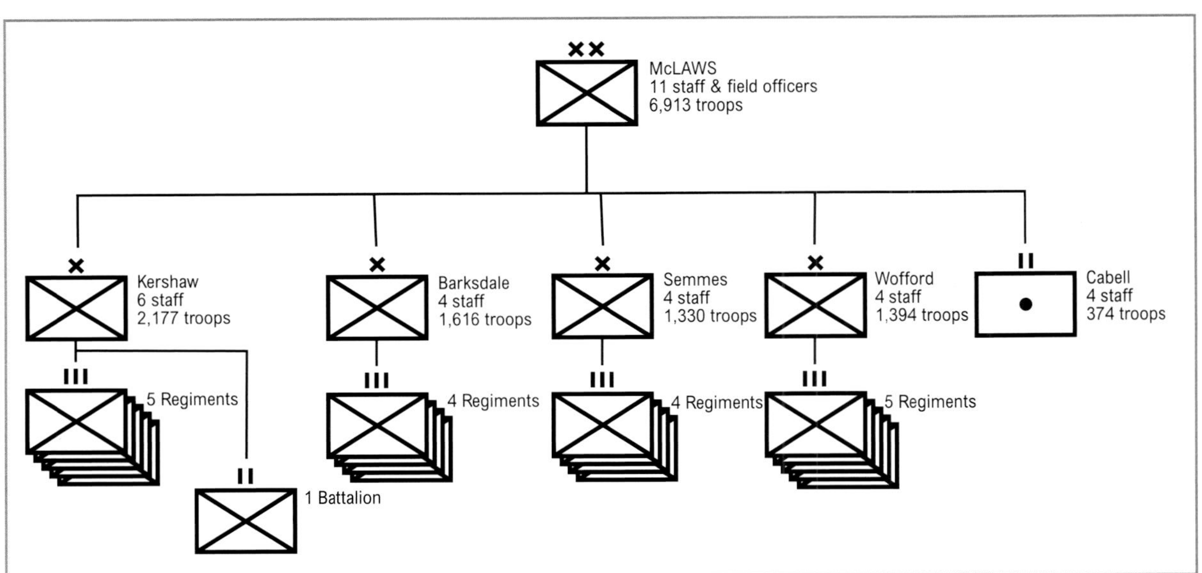

Kershaw's Brigade

Brigadier-General Joseph Kershaw's Brigade led the march of McLaws' Division to Seminary Ridge. At Pitzer's School House it turned left and proceeded toward the Peach Orchard. During this portion of the march, General Longstreet rode up and ordered Kershaw to attack the Peach Orchard and

Brigadier-General Joseph Brevard Kershaw and his men performed gallantly despite a blunder-ridden divisional deployment that exposed them to devastating flanking fire. (MARS)

KERSHAW'S BRIGADE
Brigadier-General Joseph Brevard Kershaw

2nd South Carolina Volunteer Regiment
Colonel John Doby Kennedy/
Lieutenant-Colonel Franklin Gaillard
3rd South Carolina Volunteer Regiment
Major Robert Clayton Maffett
7th South Carolina Volunteer Regiment
Lieutenant-Colonel Elbert Bland/
Colonel David Wyatt Aiken
8th South Carolina Volunteer Regiment
Colonel John Williford Henagan/
Lieutenant-Colonel Axalla John Hoole/
Major Donald Mc. McLeod/
Captain S.G. Malloy
15th South Carolina Volunteer Regiment
Colonel William Davie de Saussure/
Major William Murena Gist
3rd South Carolina Volunteer Battalion
Lieutenant-Colonel William George Rice

2nd South Carolina Volunteer Infantry Regiment

Co. A	Governor's Guards
Co. B	Butler Guards
Co. C	Columbia Grays
Co. D	Sumter Volunteers
Co. E	Camden Volunteers
Co. F	Secession Guard
Co. G	Flat Rock Guards
Co. H	Lancaster Invincibles
Co. I	Palmetto Guard
Co. K	Brooks Guard Volunteers

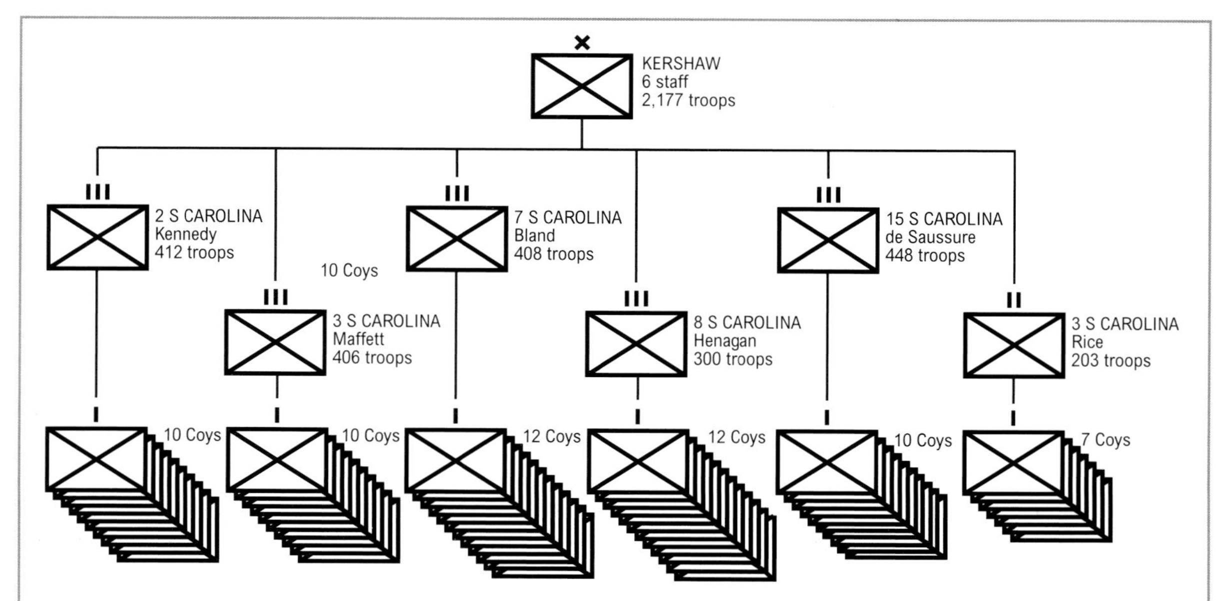

3rd South Carolina Volunteer Infantry Regiment

Co. A	State Guards
Co. B	Williams Guards
Co. C	Pickens Guards
Co. D	Cross Anchors
Co. E	Quitman Rifles
Co. F	Name not available
Co. G	Laurens Briars
Co. H	Name not available
Co. I	Musgrove Volunteers
Co. K	Blackstock Volunteers

turn the enemy flank. At about 1500 hrs the brigade entered an open field where Kershaw could see the enemy dispositions. He immediately ordered his troops to file to the right and form a battle line under cover of his skirmishers.

While the brigade deployed, Kershaw examined the Federal position. What he saw appalled him: a 'superior force in the orchard, supported by artillery, with a main line of battle entrenched in the rear and extending to and upon the rocky mountain (Little Round Top) to his left beyond the point at which his flank had supposed to rest.' If Kershaw obeyed orders, his men would have to storm the Peach Orchard and then wheel and present his brigade's flank and rear to the enemy.

Kershaw sent a courier with this information to McLaws. Meanwhile the remainder of the division was deploying on his left flank and to his rear. A further series of orders from both Longstreet and McLaws

7th South Carolina Volunteer Infantry Regiment

Cos. A through M. All Company names not available.

8th South Carolina Volunteer Infantry Regiment

Cos. A through M. All Company names not available.

modified Kershaw's original instructions. He was to wait until Hood's Division advanced and engaged. Then he would swing around the Peach Orchard and attack. He was to maintain contact and cooperate with Hood on his right. 'It was understood' that Hood 'was to sweep down the enemy's line in a direction perpendicular to' Kershaw's start line. Barksdale was to move at the same time as Kershaw and conform to his movements.

15th South Carolina Volunteer Infantry Regiment

Co. A	Columbia Rifles
Co. B	Gist Guards
Co. C	Lexington Guards
Co. D	Kershaw Guards
Co. E	Monticello Guards
Co. F	Thicketty Rifles
Co. G	Williamsburg Riflemen
Co. H	Mount Tabor Co.
Co. I	Dutch Fork Guards
Co. K	Dorn's Invincibles

3rd South Carolina Volunteer Battalion

Co. A	Captain J.M. Townsend's Co.
Co. B	Captain J.G. Williams' Co.
Co. C	Captain J.S. Shumate's Co.
Co. D	Calhoun Light Infantry
Co. E	Captain M.M. Hunter's Co.
Co. F	Harper Rifles
Co. G	Aiken Guards

Barksdale's Brigade

McLaws' Division deployed with two brigades forward and two in support. Barksdale's Mississippians were in the front left rank of the division with Kershaw's South Carolina Brigade on the right. Kershaw reported, 'I was told that Barksdale would move with me and conform to my movements.'

Barksdale's Brigade formed at about 1530 hrs along a stone wall on the front slope of Seminary Ridge. From left to right were the 18th, 13th, 17th, and 21st Mississippi. From this position they could clearly see the yankees of Sickles' III Corps in the Peach Orchard. They endured an anxious wait while Hood's Division began the offensive at about 1600 hrs.

Barksdale summoned his regimental commanders

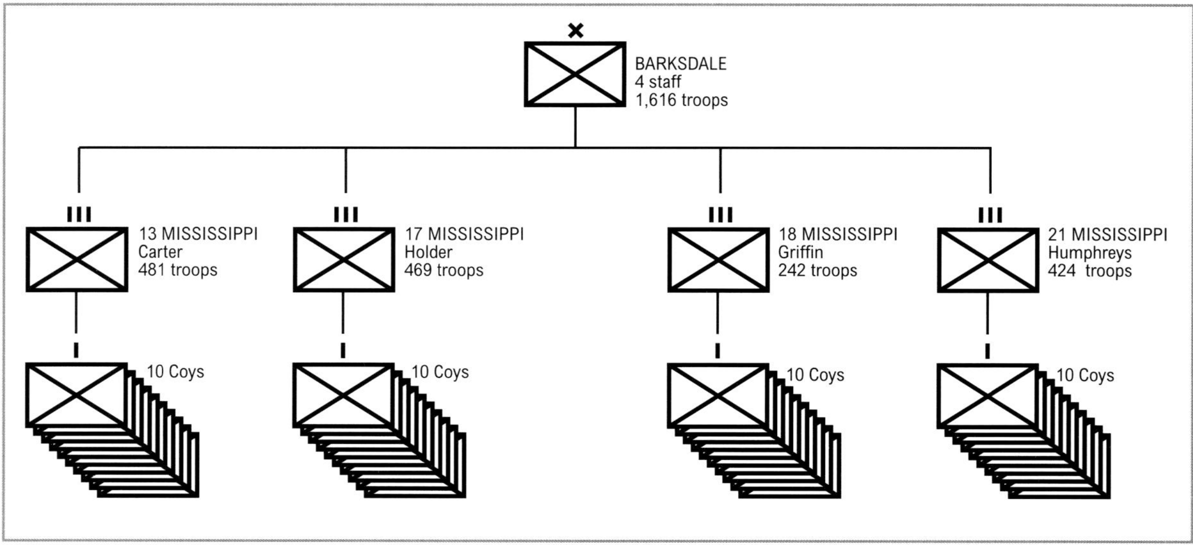

Brigadier-General William Barksdale, one-time lawyer, editor and Congressman, at age 42 was a hard-charging front-line leader whose conduct inspired his Mississippi troops. (MARS)

BARKSDALE'S BRIGADE
Brigadier-General William Barksdale/
Colonel Benjamin Grubb Humphreys

13th Mississippi Volunteer Infantry Regiment
Colonel James W. Carter/
Major Kennon McElroy/
Successor 's name not available
17th Mississippi Volunteer Infantry Regiment
Colonel William Dunbar Holder/
Lieutenant-Colonel John Calvin Fiser/
Successor's name not available
18th Mississippi Volunteer Infantry Regiment
Colonel Thomas M. Griffin/
Lieutenant-Colonel William Henry Luse/
Major George B. Gerald
21st Mississippi Volunteer Infantry Regiment
Colonel Benjamin Grubb Humphreys/
Major Daniel N. Moody

13th Mississippi Volunteer Infantry Regiment

Co. A	Winston Guards
Co. B	Wayne Rifles
Co. C	Kemper Legion
Co. D	Newton Rifles
Co. E	Alamutcha Infantry
Co. F	Lauderdale Zouaves
Co. G	The Secessionists
Co. H	Spartan Band
Co. I	Minute Men of Attala
Co. K	Pettus Guards

and told them that only he and his staff would remain mounted during the charge. Then, pointing to the Peach Orchard, he said, 'The line before you must be broken today so let every officer and man animate his comrades by his personal presence in the front line.'

Barksdale would lead by example, and because he remained mounted he would therefore become a prominent target.

17th Mississippi Volunteer Infantry Regiment

Co. A	Buena Vista Rifles
Co. B	Mississippi Rangers
Co. C	Quitman Grays
Co. D	Rough and Ready
Co. E	Burnsville Blues
Co. F	Sam Benton Rifles
Co. G	Confederate Guards
Co. H	Panola Vindicators
Co. I	Pettus Rifles
Co. K	Magnolia Guards

18th Mississippi Volunteer Infantry Regiment

Co. A	Confederate Rifles
Co. B	Benton Rifles
Co. C	Confederates
Co. D	Hamer Rifles
Co. E	Mississippi College Rifles
Co. F	McClung Rifles
Co. G	Camden Rifles
Co. H	Brown Rifles
Co. I	Beauregard Rifles
Co. K	Burt Rifles

21st Mississippi Volunteer Infantry Regiment

Co. A	Volunteer Southrons
Co. C	Stephens' Rifles
Co. D	Jeff Davis Guards
Co. E	Hurricane Rifles
Co. F	Tallahatchie Rifles
Co. G	Madison Guards
Co. H	Warren Volunteers
Co. I	Sunflower Guards
Co. K	New Albany Grays
Co. L	Vicksburg Confederates

Semmes' Brigade

Brigadier-General Paul Semmes' Georgia Brigade marched south from Herr Ridge with McLaws' column. It reached its assigned position in front of Biesecker's Woods at about 1530 hrs. Semmes deployed his men in the division's

Brigadier-General Paul Jones Semmes, former banker and planter from Georgia, at 48 had proved himself a brave and able commander. He typically wore a red turban and sash as part of his elegant battle dress. (MARS)

SEMMES' BRIGADE
Brigadier-General Paul Jones Semmes/
Colonel Goode Bryan

10th Regiment Georgia Volunteer Infantry
Colonel John B. Weems/
Successor's name not available
50th Regiment Georgia Volunteer Infantry
Colonel William R. Manning/
Lieutenant-Colonel Francis Kearse/
Captain Peter A.S. McGlashan/
Major William Oliver Fleming
51st Regiment Georgia Volunteer Infantry
Colonel Edward Ball
53rd Regiment Georgia Volunteer Infantry
Colonel James Phillip Simms

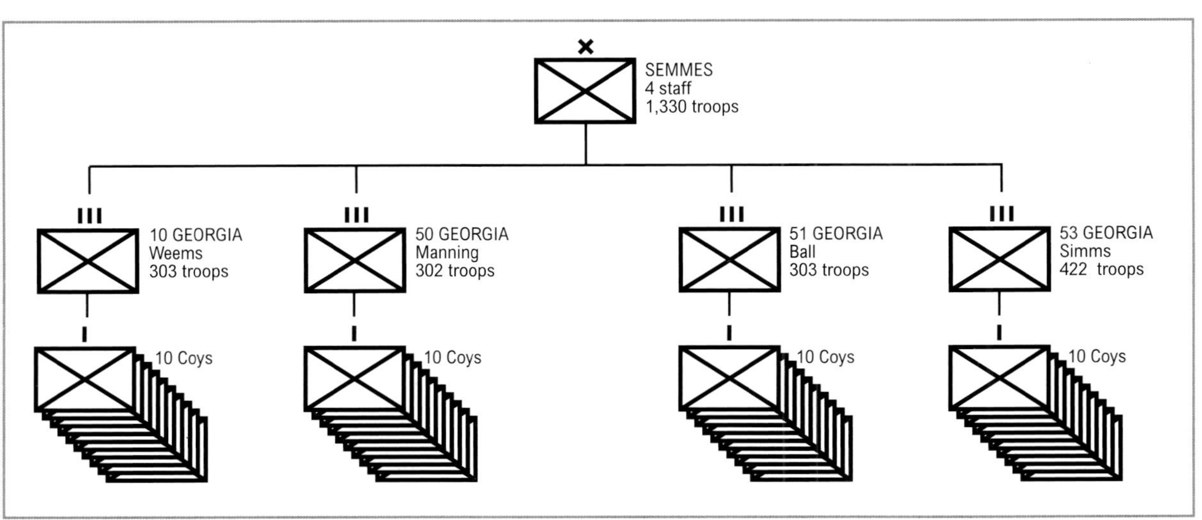

10th Regiment Georgia Volunteer Infantry	
Co. A	Confederate Sentinels
Co. B	Letcher Guards
Co. C	Chattahoochee Beauregards
Co. D	Independent Blues
Co. E	Clayton Sharpshooters
Co. F	Thompson Guards
Co. G	Name not available
Co. H	Wilcox County Rifles
Co. I	Fayette Grey Guards
Co. K	Davis Musketeers Guards

51st Regiment Georgia Volunteer Infantry	
Co. A	Early Volunteers
Co. B	Lee Guards
Co. C	Mitchell Vanguard
Co. D	Miller Guards
Co. E	Pochilla Guard
Co. F	Terrell Infantry
Co. G	Harrison Volunteers
Co. H	Randolph Rangers
Co. I	Clay Volunteers
Co. K	Dougherty Guards

second line about 150 yards behind the left flank of Kershaw's South Carolina Brigade. From left to right the order was: 10th Georgia; 50th Georgia; 51st Georgia and 53rd Georgia.

McLaws ordered Semmes to preserve his alignment and the spacing between brigades when he charged. When Kershaw advanced at about 1700 hrs, Semmes' Brigade initially remained in reserve.

50th Regiment Georgia Volunteer Infantry	
Co. A	Satilla Rangers
Co. B	Ware Volunteers
Co. C	Coffee Guards
Co. D	Valdosta Guards
Co. E	Thomas County Rangers
Co. F	Decatur Infantry
Co. G	Clinch Volunteers
Co. H	Colquitt Marksmen
Co. I	Berrien County Light Infantry
Co. K	Brooks Volunteers

53rd Regiment Georgia Volunteer Infantry	
Co. A	Doyal Volunteers
Co. B	Couth River Farmers
Co. C	Fayette Planters
Co. D	Name not available
Co. E	Newton Anderson Guards
Co. F	Dixie Guards
Co. G	Georgia Rebels
Co. H	Dixie Volunteers
Co. I	Jeff Davis Riflemen
Co. K	Quitman Guards

Wofford's Brigade

Shortly after 1300 hrs Wofford's Georgia Brigade moved to follow the division's leading elements on the march to the supposed Federal flank. It approached Black Horse Tavern, the spot from where McLaws and Longstreet had conducted a long-range visual reconnaissance. In order to avoid detection, the two senior officers ordered a counter-march. The brigade passed by 'the point at which we had before halted', crossed Herr Ridge, and then followed Willoughby Run southward in columns of companies. McLaws related, 'After very considerable difficulty, owing to the rough character of the country in places and the fences and ditches we had to cross' the men completed the counter-march. It had taken about four

WOFFORD'S BRIGADE
Brigadier-General William Tatum Wofford

16th Regiment Georgia Volunteer Infantry
Colonel Goode Bryan/
Successor's name not available
18th Regiment Georgia Volunteer Infantry
Lieutenant-Colonel Solon Zackery Ruff
24th Regiment Georgia Volunteer Infantry
Colonel Robert McMillan
Phillip's (Georgia) Legion Infantry
Lieutenant-Colonel Elihu Sandy Barclay, Jr.
Cobb's (Georgia) Legion Infantry
Lieutenant-Colonel Luther Judson Glenn

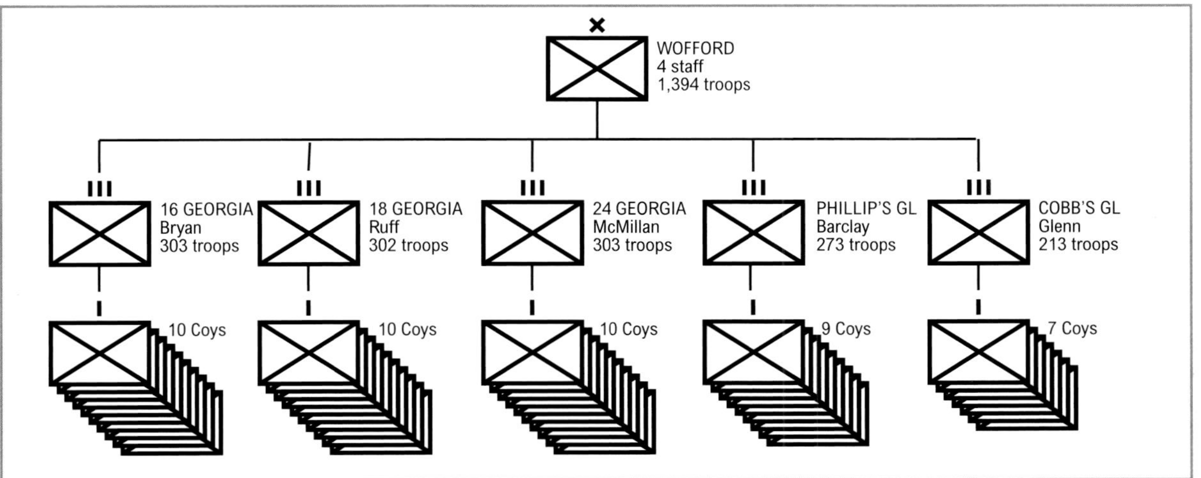

Brigadier-General William Tatum Wofford rose from difficult circumstances to prosper as a lawyer, planter, editor and Unionist state legislator. The 39-year-old Georgian was daring and ambitious. (MARS)

hours to move laterally three miles.

In a narrow, company-wide column, the brigade proceeded to the edge of Pitzer's Woods facing the Peach Orchard. After deploying his leading two brigades, McLaws rode back 'to quicken the march of those in the rear.' Since the column extended one and one-half miles, it still proved time-consuming to deploy it 'across the country broken by fences and ditches.'

16th Regiment Georgia Volunteer Infantry

Co. A	Madison County Greys
Co. B	Jackson County Volunteers
Co. C	Hartwell Infantry
Co. D	Danielsville Guards
Co. E	Cobb Infantry
Co. F	Name not available
Co. G	Name not available
Co. H	Name not available
Co. I	Name not available
Co. K	Name not available

18th Regiment Georgia Volunteer Infantry

Co. A	Acworth Infantry
Co. B	Newton Rifles
Co. C	Jackson County Volunteers
Co. D	Davis Invincibles
Co. E	Stephens Infantry
Co. F	Davis Guards
Co. G	Lewis Volunteers
Co. H	Rowland Highlanders
Co. I	Dooly Light Infantry
Co. K	Rowland Infantry

Battle flag of Cobb's Georgia Infantry Legion.

Wofford's Brigade deployed behind Barksdale in the order from right to left, 16th Georgia, 18th Georgia, 24th Georgia, Cobb's Legion, Phillips' Legion. At about 1700 hrs the brigade started forward. An eyewitness

Phillips' Georgia Infantry Legion

Co. A	Green County Rifles
Co. B	Dalton Guards
Co. C	Habersham Rifles
Co. D	Polk Rifles
Co. E	Blue Ridge Rifles
Co. F	Lochrane Guards
Co. L	Blackwell Volunteers
Co. M	Name not available
Co. O	Marrietta Guard

24th Regiment Georgia Volunteer Infantry

Co. A	Independent Volunteers
Co. B	Name not available
Co. C	White County Marksmen
Co. D	Hiawassee Volunteers
Co. E	Rabun Gap Riflemen
Co. F	Gwinett Independent Blues
Co. G	Name not available
Co. H	Currahee Rangers
Co. I	Glade Guards Volunteer Rifles
Co. K	McMillan Guards

saw Wofford and recalled, 'Oh, he was a grand sight...Long may Gen. Wofford live to lead his men to victory.'

Cobb's Georgia Legion

Co. A	Lamar Infantry
Co. B	Bowdon Volunteers
Co. C	Stephens Rifles
Co. D	Mell Rifles
Co. E	Burk's Poirths Volunteers
Co. F	Invincibles
Co. G	Name not available

Divisional Artillery - Cabell's Battalion of Artillery

When Colonel Edward Porter Alexander received the assignment to take tactical control of I Corps artillery, he rode along Seminary Ridge with the army's Chief of Artillery, General Pendleton, to examine the lie of the land. He then rode north to find his command. Alexander led an artillery column headed by Cabell's Battalion to the Black Horse Tavern. It crossed the Fairfield Road and continued south. In order to avoid being seen from the Federal signal station on Little Round Top, the column turned into the fields to bypass an exposed crest. The column returned to the road and proceeded past Pitzer's Schoolhouse before pulling over to take shelter in the shade. Here it waited for the infantry.

When the infantry arrived at about 1500 hrs, the battalion continued to its firing positions on the east slope of Seminary Ridge. According to Cabell: 'On our right, and slightly in front, the enemy occupied a rocky mountain with several batteries, and directly in front, about 600 or 700 yards distant, were a large number of batteries, occupying a peach orchard.'

The battalion's four batteries deployed in front of Kershaw's Brigade. From right to left the order was: Fraser's Battery; McCarthy's Battery with its rifled section forward and the Napoleon section in reserve; the rifled section of Carlton's battery; Manly's Battery and the 12-pounder howitzer section of Carlton's battery. At about 1600 hrs came the order to open fire on the Federal batteries in the Peach Orchard.

BATTALION EQUIPMENT

16 Caissons
213 Horses
2 Forges
1 Battery Wagon

Cabell's Battalion of Artillery
Colonel Henry Coalter Cabell
4 Staff and Field Officers

Company A, 10th North Carolina State Troops
Ellis Light Artillery
Captain Basil Charles Manly
2 x 3-inch rifled guns
2 x 12-pounder howitzers
(131 troops present for duty equipped)

Troup Artillery (Georgia)
Captain Henry H. Carlton
2 x 10-pounder Parrott rifled guns
2 x 12-pounder howitzers
(90 troops present for duty equipped)

Pulaski Artillery (Georgia)
Captain John C. Fraser/
Lieutenant William J. Furlong/
Lieutenant Robert M. Anderson
2 x 3-inch rifled guns
2 x 10-pounder Parrott rifled guns
(63 troops present for duty equipped)

1st Richmond Howitzers (Virginia)
Captain Edward Stephens McCarthy
2 x 3-inch rifled guns
2 x 12-pounder Napoleon guns
(90 troops present for duty equipped)

I Corps – Pickett's Division

Major-General George Pickett's Division entered Chambersburg on June 27. This was the anniversary of the Battle of Gaines' Mill, a battle which had seen Pickett seriously wounded in the shoulder. Pickett required three months to heal. The Battle of Gaines' Mill had been his last significant combat experience until July 1863. He had never led a division in battle.

The division camped on the York Road about four miles south of Chambersburg. It received orders to destroy the railroad by burning the ties and 'injuring the rails as much as practicable.' For the next three days, work details set about wrecking railroad depots, workshops and public machinery while nominally guarding the army's rear. A veteran recalls how the area around the bivouac had the appearance of a desert except for 'an occasional knot of men or boys at the street corners sullenly scowling upon the "secesh"' as they went about their tasks of destruction. When a young lady delivered them 'a spicy address', the

Major-General George Edward Pickett and his division spent most of July 2 labouring towards Gettysburg under a hot sun. On arrival, Lee ordered them into camp to await further instructions. (MARS)

PICKETT'S DIVISION
(not present at Gettysburg on July 2)
Major-General George Edward Pickett

GARNETT'S BRIGADE
Brigadier-General Richard Brooke Garnett
8th Virginia Infantry Regiment
Colonel Eppa Hunton
18th Virginia Infantry Regiment
Lieutenant-Colonel Henry Alexander Carrington
19th Virginia Infantry Regiment
Colonel Henry Gantt
28th Virginia Infantry Regiment
Colonel Robert Clotworthy Allen
56th Virginia Infantry Regiment
Colonel William Dabney Stuart

KEMPER'S BRIGADE
Brigadier-General James Lawson Kemper
1st Virginia Infantry Regiment
Colonel Lewis Burwell Williams, Jr.
3rd Virginia Infantry Regiment
Colonel Joseph Mayo, Jr.
7th Virginia Infantry Regiment
Colonel Waller Tazewell Patton
11th Virginia Infantry Regiment
Major Kirkwood Otey
24th Virginia Infantry Regiment
Colonel William Richard Terry

ARMISTEAD'S BRIGADE
Brigadier-General Lewis Addison Armistead
9th Virginia Infantry Regiment
Major John Crowder Owens
14th Virginia Infantry Regiment
Colonel James Gregory Hodges
38th Virginia Infantry Regiment
Colonel Edward Claxton Edmonds
53rd Virginia Infantry Regiment
Colonel William Roane Aylett
57th Virginia Infantry Regiment
Colonel John Bowie Magruder

38th VIRGINIA LIGHT ARTILLERY BATTALION
Major James Dearing
Co A., Fauquier Artillery (Virginia)
Captain Robert Mackey Stribling
Co.C., Hampden Artillery (Virginia)
Captain William Henderson Caskie
Co.B., Richmond Fayette Artillery (Virginia)
Captain Miles Cary Macon
Co.D., Lynchburg Artillery (Virginia)
Captain Joseph Grey Blount

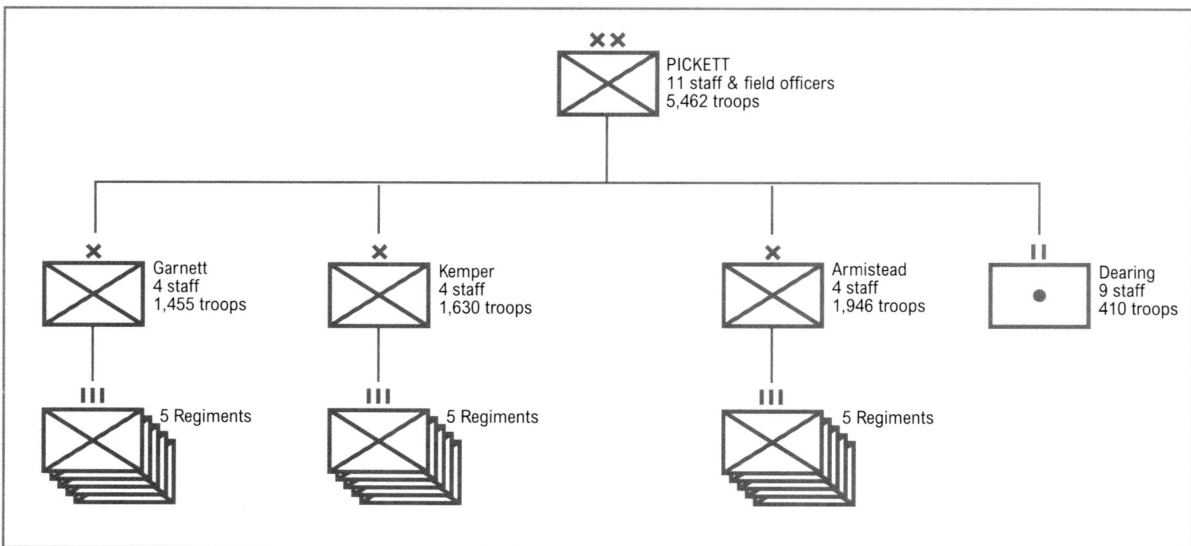

Virginians replied by having a band play Dixie.

Finally an overdue cavalry force commanded by Brigadier-General Imboden arrived late on July 1 to relieve Pickett's Division of guard duty. At around 0200 hrs on July 2 the division left camp and set off for Gettysburg.

Under a hot July sun, the division 'pushed on as fast as possible.' It marched along the turnpike and approached the Cashtown Gap around noon. Units paused for a ten-minute break at the crest. Northern 'bushwhackers', probably irate citizens or boys seeking excitement, fired on the column from the safety of the nearby heights. They inflicted no losses.

The vanguard's march resumed at around 1300 hrs. On the eastern side of the gap, soldiers heard the sound of heavy firing towards Gettysburg. The leading units neared Gettysburg at about 1600 hrs. General Pickett rode ahead to report to Longstreet personally and sent an aide to tell Lee that the division was weary from its march. Lee replied 'Tell General Pickett I shall not want him this evening, to let his men rest, and I will send him word when I want them.'

Early on July 2, in hot and sultry weather, Pickett started his march east. Greatly delayed by the army's trains, the centre of his column reached Cashtown Gap about noon where it took a 10-minute break. Thereafter his forced-march to Gettysburg was much more rapid.

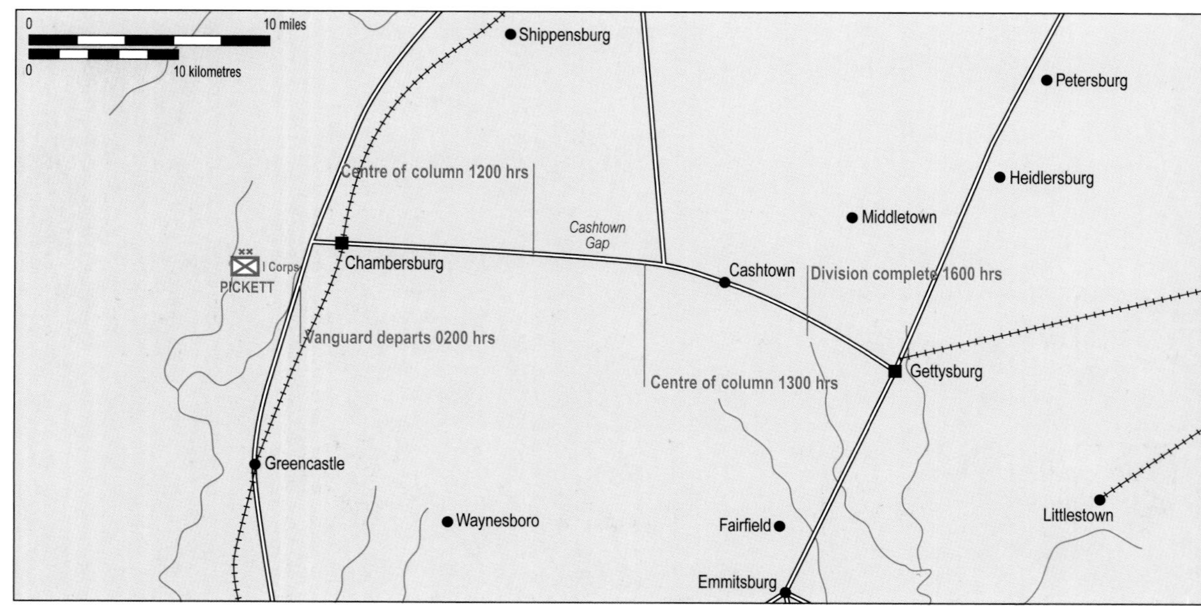

I Corps – Hood's Division

On the morning of July 2, Hood's Division departed its camp at Marsh Creek and moved up to the fields west of Seminary Ridge near the Chambersburg Pike. Law's Brigade was marching from New Guilford to join the division. Hood rode ahead to confer with Longstreet and Lee. He learned that he was to follow McLaws' Division, align his men astride the Union flank, and attack up the Emmitsburg Road towards Gettysburg.

Around noon the flank march began. The division marched along a small stream to Marsh Run and onto a road that took them toward Black Horse Tavern. Here the route converged with a side road on which McLaws was marching. A traffic jam occurred.

According to McLaws, Hood, 'in his eagerness for the fray (and he bears the character of always being so), had pressed on his division behind mine so that it lapped considerably, creating confusion in the counter-march.'

Major-General John Bell Hood had misgivings about the plan of attack and failed to persuade Longstreet to change it. Nevertheless, he gallantly led his men into battle and was seriously wounded. (Library of Congress)

HOOD'S DIVISION
Major-General John Bell Hood/
Brigadier-General Evander McIvor Law

Law's Brigade - 1,929 troops
Anderson's Brigade - 1,864 troops
Robertson's Brigade - 1,729 troops
Benning's Brigade - 1,416 troops
Henry's Artillery Battalion - 394 troops

Longstreet suggested that since Hood's men were intermingled with McLaws' troops, Hood should 'counter-march first and lead in the attack.' McLaws replied, 'General, as I started in the lead, let me continue so.'

Longstreet concurred. By virtue of this ridiculous decision, Hood's men stood idle while McLaws' troops shouldered their way past. By 1600 hrs the division was finally in position in Biesecker's Woods. It formed in two lines of two brigades each and waited for the signal to charge.

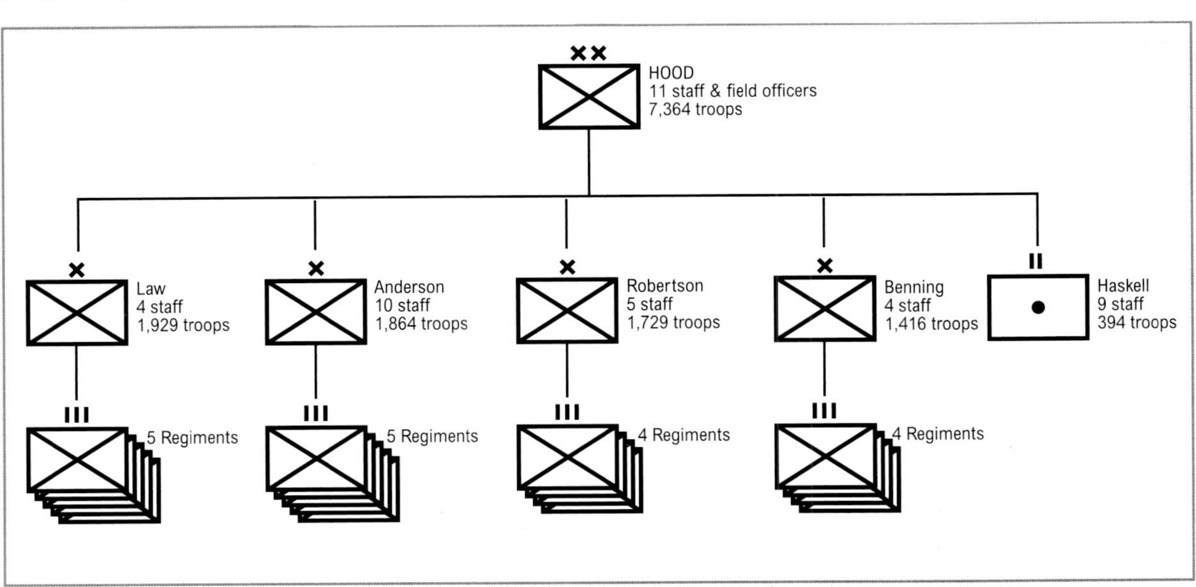

Law's Brigade

While Hood's Division marched towards Gettysburg on July 1, Law's Alabama Brigade remained at New Guilford in the Cumberland Valley to protect the army's rear. Normally this would have been a duty for the cavalry, but Stuart's disappearance compelled the infantry to undertake it. The Alabamians enjoyed their rest by dining on a local farmer's hogs and using the surplus meat to cook rations.

The brigade received a recall order late on July 1. It began its march to Gettysburg at 0300 hrs the next day. Because the road was clear of traffic, the men made good time and joined Hood's Division on the Chambersburg Pike at about 1400 hrs, having covered 25 miles in 11 hours. Longstreet later praised

LAW'S BRIGADE
Brigadier-General Evander McIvor Law/
Colonel James Lawrence Sheffield

4th Alabama Infantry Regiment
Colonel Pinckney Downie Bowles
15th Alabama Infantry Regiment
Colonel William Calvin Oates/
Captain Blanton Abram Hill
44th Alabama Infantry Regiment
Colonel William Flake Perry/
Major George Walton Cary
47th Alabama Infantry Regiment
Colonel James W. Jackson/
Lieutenant-Colonel Michael Jefferson Bulger/
Major James McDonald Campbell
48th Alabama Infantry Regiment
Colonel James Lawrence Sheffield/
Captain T.J. Eubanks

4th Alabama Volunteer Infantry Regiment

Co. A	Governor's Guard
Co. B	Name not available
Co. C	Name not available
Co. D	Canebrake Rifle Guards
Co. E	Conecuh Guards
Co. F	Name not available
Co. G	Marion Light Infantry
Co. H	Lauderdale Volunteer Dragoons
Co. I	North Alabamians
Co. K	Larkinsville Guards

Brigadier-General Evander McIvor Law and his brigade marched 24 miles to reach the battlefield, then endured several hours of backtracking and repositioning before they could join the fighting on Little Round Top. (MARS)

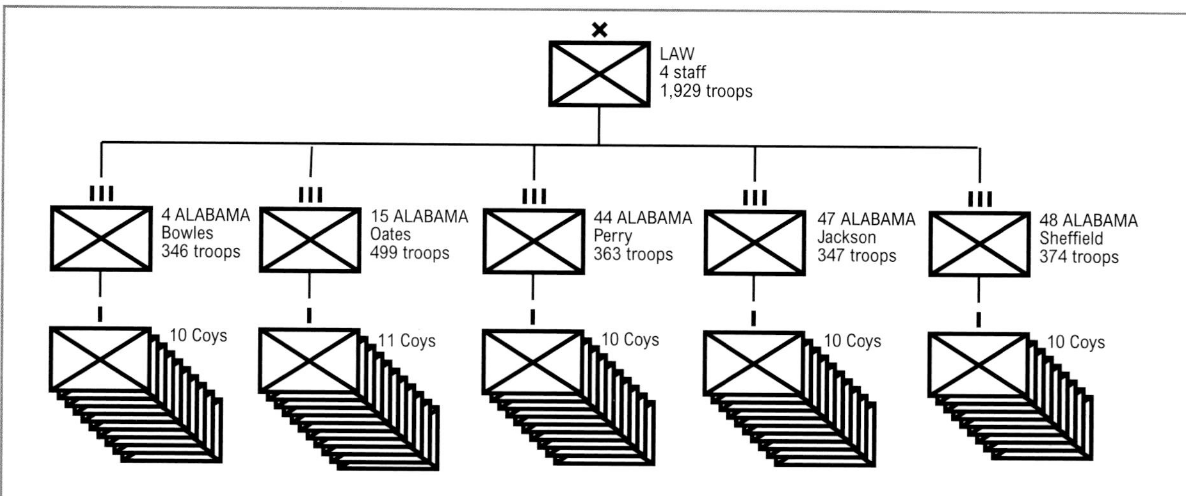

15th Alabama Volunteer Infantry Regiment

Co. A Cantey Rifles
Co. B Midway Southern Guards
Co. C Name not available
Co. D Fort Browder Roughs
Co. E Name not available
Co. F Brundridge Guards
Co. G Henry Pioneers
Co. H Glenville Guards
Co. I Name not available
Co. K Eufaula City Guard
Co. L Name not available

the men, calling their effort 'the best marching done in either army to reach the field of Gettysburg.'

With very little time to rest, the brigade participated in the flank march designed to place the division on the Union flank. It ended up on the extreme Confederate right, east of the Emmitsburg Road and opposite Bushman's Woods and Round Top and deployed behind a stone wall.

While the brigade deployed, Law dispatched scouts forward. They learned that Round Top was undefended and from prisoners Law learned that a weakly guarded wagon train was parked behind Round Top. Law claimed that he tried to persuade Hood to revise the division's attack. In the event, although he had orders to wheel left and charge, Law resolved to disobey and advance straight toward Devil's Den and the Round Tops.

44th Alabama Volunteer Infantry Regiment

Cos. A through K. All Company names not available.

47th Alabama Volunteer Infantry Regiment

Co. A Name not available
Co. B Tallapoosa Light Infantry
Co. C Jeff Holly Guards
Co. D Name not available
Co. E. Name not available
Co. F Name not available
Co. G Name not available
Co. H Name not available
Co. I Chambers' Infantry
Co. K Goldthwaith Grays

48th Alabama Volunteer Infantry Regiment

Co. A Jackson Boys
Co. B Wills Valley Guards
Co. C Mountain Rangers
Co. D Sheffield Guards
Co. E The Jacksonians
Co. F Jeff Davis Boys
Co. G Elisha King Guards
Co. H Cherokee Grays
Co. I Newman Pound Guards
Co. K Moore Rifles

Anderson's Brigade

Brigadier-General George T. ('Tige', a nickname reputedly given in lieu of 'Tiger') Anderson was to have only a brief role at Gettysburg before receiving a painful wound causing him to yield command to his senior colonel. A Georgia native, he had served as a lieutenant with a Georgia cavalry company during the Mexican War. Thereafter he secured a commission in the Regular Army before resigning in 1858.

Elected colonel of the 11th Georgia in 1861, he had led a brigade during the Seven Days' and Maryland Campaigns. He became a brigadier-general

Brigadier-General George Thomas 'Tige' Anderson, 39, a propertied Georgian, had a civilian college education and served in the cavalry during and after the Mexican War. Still unproven to his superiors, he won the hearts of his men. (MARS)

ANDERSON'S BRIGADE
Brigadier-General George Thomas Anderson/
Lieutenant-Colonel William Luffman

7th Regiment Georgia Volunteer Infantry
Colonel William Wilkinson White
8th Regiment Georgia Volunteer Infantry
Colonel John R. Towers
9th Regiment Georgia Volunteer Infantry
Lieutenant-Colonel John Clark Mounger/
Major William M. Jones/
Captain George Hillyer
11th Regiment Georgia Volunteer Infantry
Colonel Francis Hamilton Little/
Lieutenant-Colonel William Luffman/
Major Henry D. McDaniel/
Captain William H. Mitchell
59th Regiment Georgia Volunteer Infantry
Colonel William A. Jackson Brown/
Major Bolivar Hopkins Gee/
Captain Maston Green Bass

in November 1862.

Anderson's Brigade participated in Longstreet's flank march on July 2. According to Colonel William White, who was to command the brigade after 'Tige' Anderson was wounded: 'The scene of action was reached by a march of several miles under a broiling sun, and, a portion of the way, a terrific fire of the enemy's batteries. The position of the brigade was on the extreme left of Hood's division, and, when ordered to advance on the enemy's position, was to the rear, and supporting the Texas Brigade.'

7th Regiment Georgia Volunteer Infantry

Co. A	Name not available
Co. B	Name not available
Co. C	Powers Rifles
Co. D	Name not available
Co. E	Name not available
Co. F	Name not available
Co. G	Name not available
Co. H	Roswell Guards
Co. I	Cobb Mountaineers
Co. K	Davis Infantry

Because the 7th Georgia had to be detached to 'watch the movements of the enemy's cavalry' – yet another diminution of infantry strength on a duty that should have been performed by Stuart's cavalry – only four regiments were in the battle line. These deployed behind Robertson's Texas Brigade.

General Robertson described the scene: 'On

8th Regiment Georgia Volunteer Infantry

Co. A	Rome Light Guards
Co. B	Oglethorpe Light Infantry
Co. C	Macon Guards
Co. D	Echols' Guards
Co. E	Miller Rifles
Co. F	Atlanta Greys
Co. G	Pulaski Volunteers
Co. H	Floyd Infantry
Co. I	Stephens Light Guards
Co. K	Oglethorpe Rifles

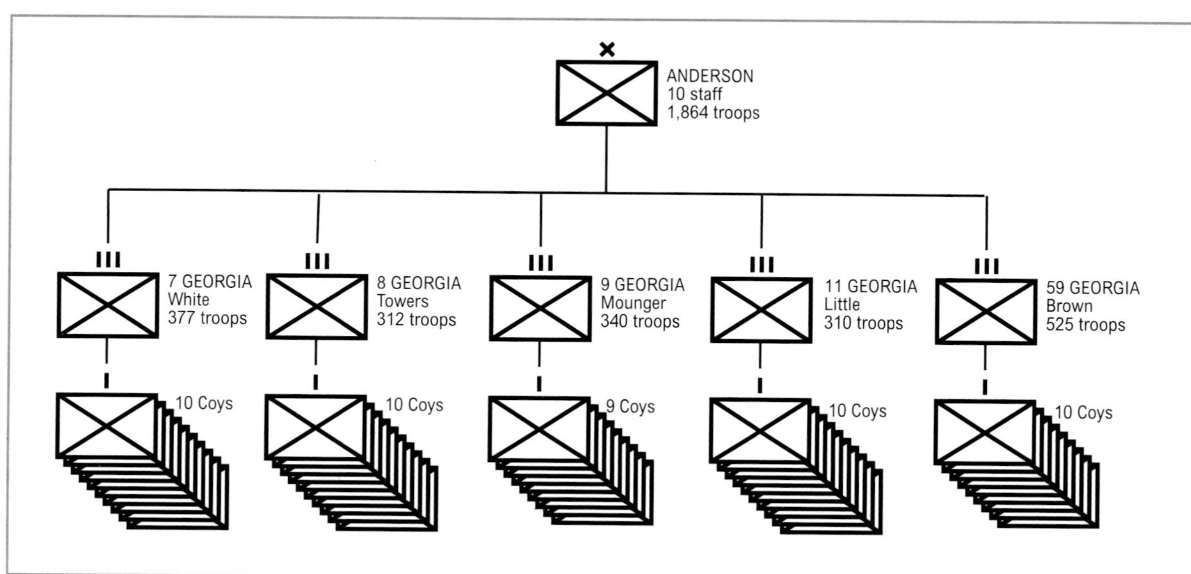

9th Regiment Georgia Volunteer Infantry

Co. B	Chattanooga Volunteers
Co. C	Hillyer Rifles
Co. D	Fort Gaines Guards
Co. E	Talbot Guards
Co. F	Baldwin County Volunteers
Co. G	Lafayette Volunteers
Co. H	Brook County Rifles
Co. I	Toombs Guards
Co. K	Americus Volunteer Rifles

11th Regiment Georgia Volunteer Infantry

Co. A	Gainsville Light Infantry
Co. B	Name not available
Co. C	Name not available
Co. D	Name not available
Co. E	Name not available
Co. F	Gilmer Volunteers
Co. G	Gilmer Lions
Co. H	Walton Infantry
Co. I	Gilmer Tigers/Quitman Greys
Co. K	Houston Volunteers

59th Regiment Georgia Volunteer Infantry

Co. A	Confederate Volunteers
Co. B	Jackson Guards
Co. C	Arthur Greys
Co. D	Bullard Guards
Co. E	Cotton Planters Guards
Co. F	Worth Guards
Co. G	Sidney Johnston's
Co. H	Name not available
Co. I	Turner Guards
Co. K	Lockett Volunteers

emerging from the woods, their position became visible. Before us, at the distance of 600 to 800 yards, was an oblong mountain peak, or spur [Devil's Den] presenting to us a steep race, much roughened by rocks. To the right, 400 or 500 yards from the peak, was the main mountain itself [Round Top], with a side that looked almost perpendicular.' Federal artillery and infantry defended these commanding positions.

Soon after the Texas Brigade engaged, at around 1700 hrs, Anderson's Brigade, with about 1,400 men, began its charge.

Robertson's Brigade

Having lost only six men at Fredericksburg and missed the Battle of Chancellorsville because they were on detached duty at Suffolk, the Texas Brigade arrived at Gettysburg well-rested, with its regiments as numerically strong as possible. Brigadier-General Jerome Robertson had been appointed to command this crack brigade back in November 1862. The soldiers liked Robertson, calling

Brigadier-General Jerome Bonaparte Robertson, 48, began his working life as a hatter's apprentice in Kentucky. He attended medical school, fought Indians and served in the state legislature before raising a volunteer company for the Confederacy. (MOLLUS)

ROBERTSON'S BRIGADE
Brigadier-General Jerome Bonaparte Robertson/
Lieutenant-Colonel Phillip Alexander Work

3rd Arkansas Infantry Regiment
Colonel Vannoy Hartrog Manning/
Lieutenant-Colonel Robert Samuel Taylor
1st Texas Infantry Regiment
Lieutenant-Colonel Phillip Alexander Work/
Major Frederick S. Bass/
Captain D.K. Rice
4th Texas Infantry Regiment
Colonel John Cotlett Garrett Key/
Lieutenant-Colonel Benjamin F. Carter
Major John P. Bane
5th Texas Infantry Regiment
Colonel Robert Michael Powell/
Lieutenant-Colonel King Bryan/
Major Jefferson Carroll Rogers

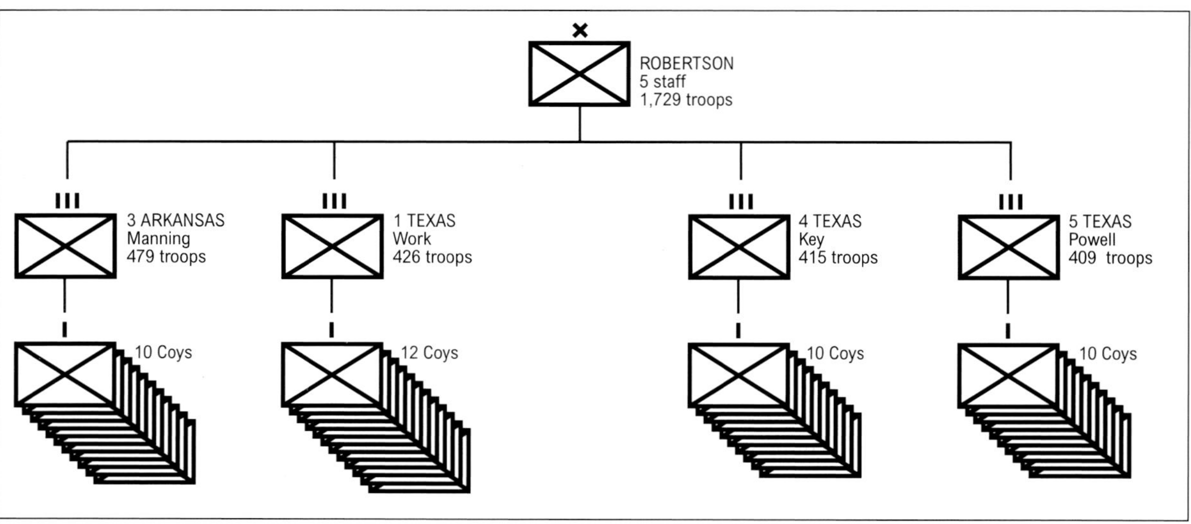

3rd Arkansas Infantry Regiment

Co. A	Arkansas Travellers
Co. B	Berlin Beauregards
Co. C	Confederate Stars
Co. D	Selma Rifles
Co. E	Champagnolle Guards
Co. F	Hot Spring Hornets
Co. G	Three Creeks Rifles
Co. H	Orphan Company
Co. I	Tulip Rifles
Co. K	Ashley Volunteers

him 'Aunt Polly' because of his conscientious care for their well-being. Gettysburg would be the first time Robertson led them in battle.

After participating in the division's frustrating march and counter-march, the Texas Brigade arrived at its jumping off position on the edge of Biesecker's Woods shortly before 1600 hrs. It formed the left front of the division's two-brigade line. The regiments deployed astride the Emmitsburg Road. South of the road was the 3rd Arkansas and 1st Texas. North of the road stood the 4th and 5th Texas.

Robertson's orders were to close his right flank on Law's Brigade while using his left flank to maintain contact with the Emmitsburg Road. Because of Law's erratic behaviour, when the brigade began its charge at 1630 hrs it was impossible to comply with this order.

1st Texas Infantry Regiment

Co. A	Marion Rifles
Co. B	Livingstone Guards
Co. C	Palmer Guards
Co. D	Star Rifles
Co. E	Corsicana Invincibles/Marshall Guards
Co. F	Woodville Rifles
Co. G	Regan Guards
Co. H	Texas Guards
Co. I	Crockett Southerns
Co. K	Daniel Boone Rifles
Co. L	Lone Star Rifles
Co. M	Name not available

4th Texas Infantry Regiment

Co. A	Hardeman Rifles
Co. B	Tom Green Rifles
Co. C	The Five Shooters
Co. D	Guadalupe Rangers
Co. E	Lone Star Guards
Co. F	Mustang Greys
Co. G	Grimes County Greys
Co. H	Porter Guards
Co. I	Naverro Rifles
Co. K	Sandy Point Mounted Rifles

5th Texas Infantry Regiment

Co. A	Bayou City Guards
Co. B	Name not available
Co. C	Leon Hunters
Co. D	Waverly Confederates
Co. E	Dixie Blues
Co. F	Washington Invincibles
Co. G	Milam Greys
Co. H	Texas Polk Rifles
Co. I	Texas Aids
Co. K	Polk County Flying Artillery

Benning's Brigade

The Georgia regiments that made up Benning's Brigade originally served under the Georgia politician Robert Toombs. Lightly engaged during the Peninsular Campaign, the brigade received a new commander when Toombs' political demands required his absence. Another politician, Brigadier-General Henry Benning, assumed command during the Second Manassas Campaign. Although unnerved early in the battle, Benning recovered his composure to acquit himself respectably. The brigade guarded 'Burnside's Bridge' during the Battle of Sharpsburg but saw only light action at Fredericksburg.

Benning, nicknamed 'Old Rock', assumed formal command in April 1863 after Toombs resigned. The brigade was detached in Suffolk during the

Brigadier-General Henry Lewis Benning, 49, was a Georgia Supreme Court justice. He opted to serve the Confederacy as a soldier rather than accept a cabinet post. (MARS)

BENNING'S BRIGADE
Brigadier-General Henry Lewis Benning

2nd Regiment Georgia Volunteer Infantry
Lieutenant-Colonel William Terrell Harris/
Major William S. Shepherd
15th Regiment Georgia Volunteer Infantry
Colonel Dudley McIver DuBose
17th Regiment Georgia Volunteer Infantry
Colonel Wesley C. Hodges
20th Regiment Georgia Volunteer Infantry
Colonel John Augustus Jones/
Lieutenant-Colonel James Daniel Waddell

2nd Regiment Georgia Volunteer Infantry

Co. A	Banks County Guards
Co. B	Georgia Blues
Co. C	Semmes Guards
Co. D	Burke Sharpshooters
Co. E	The Joe Browns
Co. F	Cherokee Brown Riflemen
Co. G	Columbus Guards
Co. H	Wright Infantry
Co. I	Buena Vista Guards
Co. K	Stewart Greys

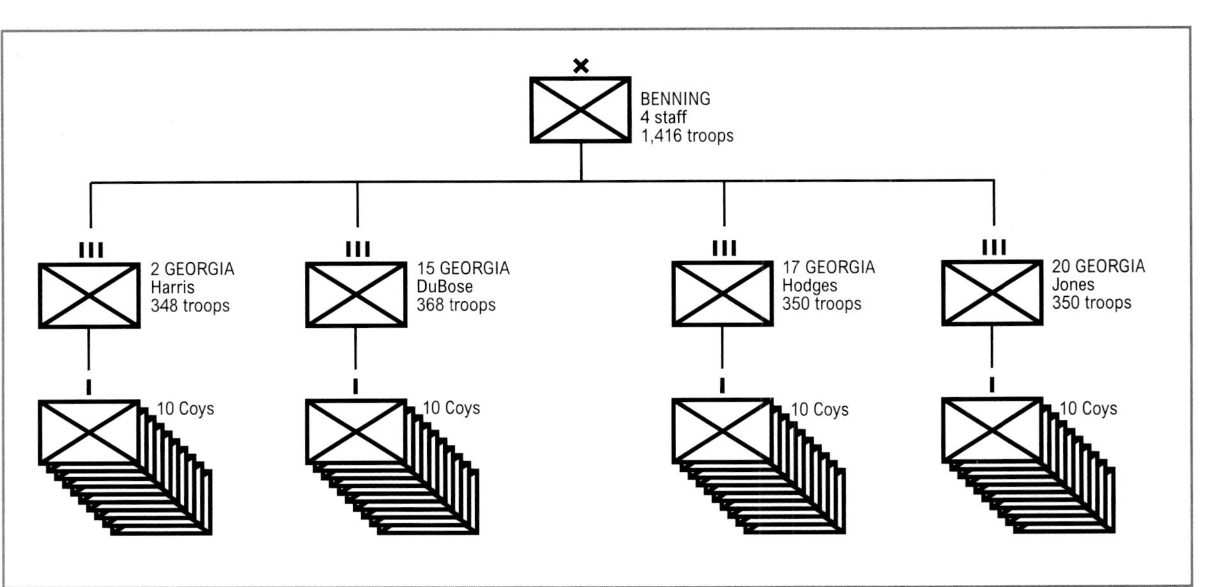

15th Regiment Georgia Volunteer Infantry

Co. A	Dehli Rangers
Co. B	Tugalo Blues
Co. C	Fireside Rangers
Co. D	Stephen Home Guards
Co. E	Hancock Volunteers
Co. F	Bowman Volunteers
Co. G	Lamar Confederates
Co. H	Pool Volunteers
Co. I	McIntosh Volunteers
Co. K	Confederate Guards

17th Regiment Georgia Volunteer Infantry

Co. A	Webster Rifles
Co. B	Name not available
Co. C	Name not available
Co. D	Decatur Grays
Co. E	Name not available
Co. F	Name not available
Co. G	Name not available
Co. H	Name not available
Co. I	Name not available
Co. K	Webster Guards

20th Regiment Georgia Volunteer Infantry

Co. A	Sparks Guards
Co. B	Border Rangers
Co. C	Jefferson Guards
Co. D	Name not available
Co. E	Whitesville Guards
Co. F	Confederate Continentals
Co. G	Name not available
Co. H	Telfair Volunteers
Co. I	Southern Guards
Co. K	Montgomery Guards

Chancellorsville Campaign. Thus its four regiments were rested and numerically strong (for veteran combat units) at Gettysburg.

Benning's Brigade formed the right rear of the divisional line. It stood about 100 yards behind Law's Brigade. The regiments deployed in Biesecker's Woods shortly before 1600 hrs. Benning's orders required him to support Law when the latter advanced. He was to maintain a 400-yard interval between brigades. Because of the trees, Benning had little notion of what lay ahead of his brigade.

Divisional Artillery - Henry's Battalion of Artillery

Major Mathias Henry's artillery battalion followed Cabell's Battalion on the flank march to the Pitzer School area. In order to support Hood's attack against the Devil's Den and Little Round Top, the battalion sought firing positions on the right of the line. Because of the rugged ground, there

Henry's Battalion of Artillery
Major John C. Haskell

Company F, 13th North Carolina Battalion Branch Artillery
Captain Alexander C. Latham
1 x 6-pounder field gun
3 x 12-pounder Napoleon guns
1 x 12-pounder howitzer
(112 troops present for duty equipped)

German Artillery (South Carolina)
Captain William K. Bachman
4 x 12-pounder Napoleon guns
(71 troops present for duty equipped)

Palmetto Light Battery (South Carolina)
Captain Hugh Richardson Garden
2 x 10-pounder Parrott rifled guns
2 x 12-pounder Napoleon guns
(63 troops present for duty equipped)

Company D, 10th North Carolina State Troops
Rowan Artillery
Captain James Reilly
2 x 3-inch rifled guns
2 x 10-pounder Parrott rifled guns
2 x 12-pounder Napoleon guns
(148 troops present for duty equipped)

was only room for two batteries to deploy.

The six guns of the Rowan Artillery deployed on a ridge crest in front of Hood's right wing. Here they had a clear shot at the Devil's Den and the Round Tops. The five guns of the Branch Artillery deployed near the Bushman farm lane in front of the Texas Brigade. They too could fire at the Devil's Den and Little Round Top as well as deliver enfilade fire north along the Emmitsburg Road against the Union infantry in the Peach Orchard. At about 1600 hrs they opened fire in an effort to find the location of the Union line.

BATTALION EQUIPMENT
16 Caissons
4 Forges
1 Battery Wagon

I Corps' Reserve Artillery

After completing an overnight march to Gettysburg, I Corps Reserve Artillery parked along the Chambersburg Pike at 0900 hrs on July 2. Following a meeting with Colonel James Walton, General Longstreet appointed Colonel Edward Alexander to tactical command of I Corps' artillery. He advised him to scout the ground and then bring his own battalion forward but leave the Washington Artillery to the rear. Longstreet told Alexander that when he moved his batteries he should avoid observation from the Federal signal station on Little Round Top. Alexander ably performed this mission, supervising the deployment of his own and the divisional artillery battalions to within 500 yards of the Union line.

Colonel James Burdge Walton
4 Staff and Field Officers

Washington Artillery Battalion (Louisiana)
Major Benjamin Franklin Eshleman
9 Staff and Field Officers
1st Company
Captain Charles W. Squires
1 x 12-pounder Napoleon gun
(77 troops present for duty equipped)
2nd Company
Captain John B. Richardson
2 x 12-pounder Napoleon guns
1 x 12-pounder howitzer
(80 troops present for duty equipped)
3rd Company
Captain Merritt B. Miller
3 x 12-pounder Napoleon guns
(92 troops present for duty equipped)
4th Company
Captain Joseph Norcom
2 x 12-pounder Napoleon guns
1 x 12-pounder howitzer
(80 troops present for duty equipped)

Alexander's Battalion of Artillery
Colonel Edward Porter Alexander
9 Staff and Field Officers
Ashland Light Artillery (Virginia)
Captain Pichegru Woolfolk, Jr./
Lieutenant James Woolfolk
4 x 12-pounder Napoleon guns
2 x 20-pounder Parrott rifled guns
(103 troops present for duty equipped)
Bedford Light Artillery (Virginia)
Captain Tyler Calhoun Jordan
4 x 3-inch rifled guns
(78 troops present for duty equipped)
Brooks Artillery (South Carolina)
Lieutenant S. Capers Gilbert
4 x 12-pounder howitzers
(71 troops present for duty equipped)
Madison Light Artillery (Louisiana)
Captain George V. Moody
4 x 24-pounder howitzers
(135 troops present for duty equipped)
Captain William Watts Parker's Company
Virginia Light Artillery
Captain William Watts Parker
3 x 3-inch rifled guns
1 x 10-pounder Parrott rifled gun
(90 troops present for duty equipped)
Captain Osmond B. Taylor's Company
Virginia Light Artillery
Captain Osmond B. Taylor
4 x 12-pounder Napoleon guns
(90 troops present for duty equipped)

THE ARMY OF NORTHERN VIRGINIA I CORPS' BATTLES

Longstreet's Corps

Longstreet's Flank March – 1200–1530 hrs

In order to have his assault divisions available in time, Longstreet ordered McLaws and Hood to march through the night. McLaws' Division reached its bivouac at Marsh Creek, about four miles from Gettysburg and chosen because it offered a good water supply, around midnight. Hood's men arrived an hour later. Colonel Walton's Artillery Reserve was much slowed by the presence of the army's trains on the Chambersburg Pike and did not reach Marsh Creek until 0900 hrs on July 2. Longstreet had also ordered Law's Brigade at New Guilford and Pickett's Division at Chambersburg to march to Gettysburg. A 25-mile speed march brought Law to Marsh Creek around noon. Pickett did not arrive in time to participate in the pending flank attack.

Longstreet reported to Lee's headquarters on Seminary Ridge around 0500 hrs. Shortly thereafter Captain Johnson returned from his reconnaissance and Lee listened to his report. Then Lee summoned Major-General Lafayette McLaws, who had just arrived, in order to brief him on the plan. Pointing to a place on the map where the Wheatfield Road crossed Seminary Ridge and to a line south of the Peach Orchard and perpendicular to the Emmitsburg Road, Lee spoke: 'General, I wish you to place your division across this road, and I wish you to get there if possible without being seen by the enemy. Can you get there?'

McLaws replied that he knew of nothing that would prevent him and said he would like to scout the position personally. Longstreet intervened. Curiously, he forbade McLaws from leaving his division. Then he ordered McLaws to deploy along a line he pointed out that was perpendicular to the one Lee had just drawn. Lee replied, 'No, General, I wish it placed just the opposite.' Clearly Longstreet was going to be a balky subordinate while supervising Lee's plan. Longstreet revealed his attitude again when he requested permission to delay the march until Law's Brigade rejoined Hood's Division.

While the two assault divisions dozed among the trees along Herr Ridge, Longstreet ordered Colonel Edward Alexander to assume tactical command of I Corps' artillery and to scout the route of the pending flank march and then move his guns. He cautioned him to stay out of view of the Federal signal station on Little Round Top. Alexander completed both tasks. The only problem came just south of Black Horse Tavern where the road lay exposed to view from Little Round Top. Alexander simply moved his guns through the adjacent fields to avoid this section of the road.

The infantry began their march sometime around noon with McLaws' Division in the van. When McLaws reached the exposed piece of road, he was flummoxed. He waited for instructions from Longstreet. For some reason he never considered following the path taken by Alexander's artillery. When McLaws halted, Hood's men marched into his rear and created a traffic jam. Irritated, Longstreet arrived to sort things out. He saw the exposed portion of the road and commented, 'This won't do. Is there no way to avoid it?'

The officers resolved to counter-march. Yet when Longstreet proposed that Hood now become the column's van, McLaws protested. Consequently, McLaws' soldiers retraced their steps and filed past Hood's motionless men. The column re-passed Herr's Ridge, followed the road that Pendleton had originally located along Willoughby Run, and regained the road leading to Pitzer's Schoolhouse. It continued a short way east before Hood's Division split off to the south to form the Confederate right flank. McLaws' men filed into position adjacent to Anderson's Division. The artillery batteries assumed firing positions in a line roughly parallel to Emmitsburg Road. The deployment was complete by about 1600 hrs.

1200 hrs	1300	1400	1500	1600	1700	1800	1900	2000	2100	2200
				32-39,67-69	40-43	91-93		70-73		

Longstreet's initial route on his covert march to the Federal left flank would have brought him, just south of Black Horse Tavern, into view from the Union signal station on Little Round Top. A time-consuming counter-march ensued, further delaying the Confederate manoeuvre, and when they reached the Emmitsburg Road they discovered Federal troops facing them deployed for battle.

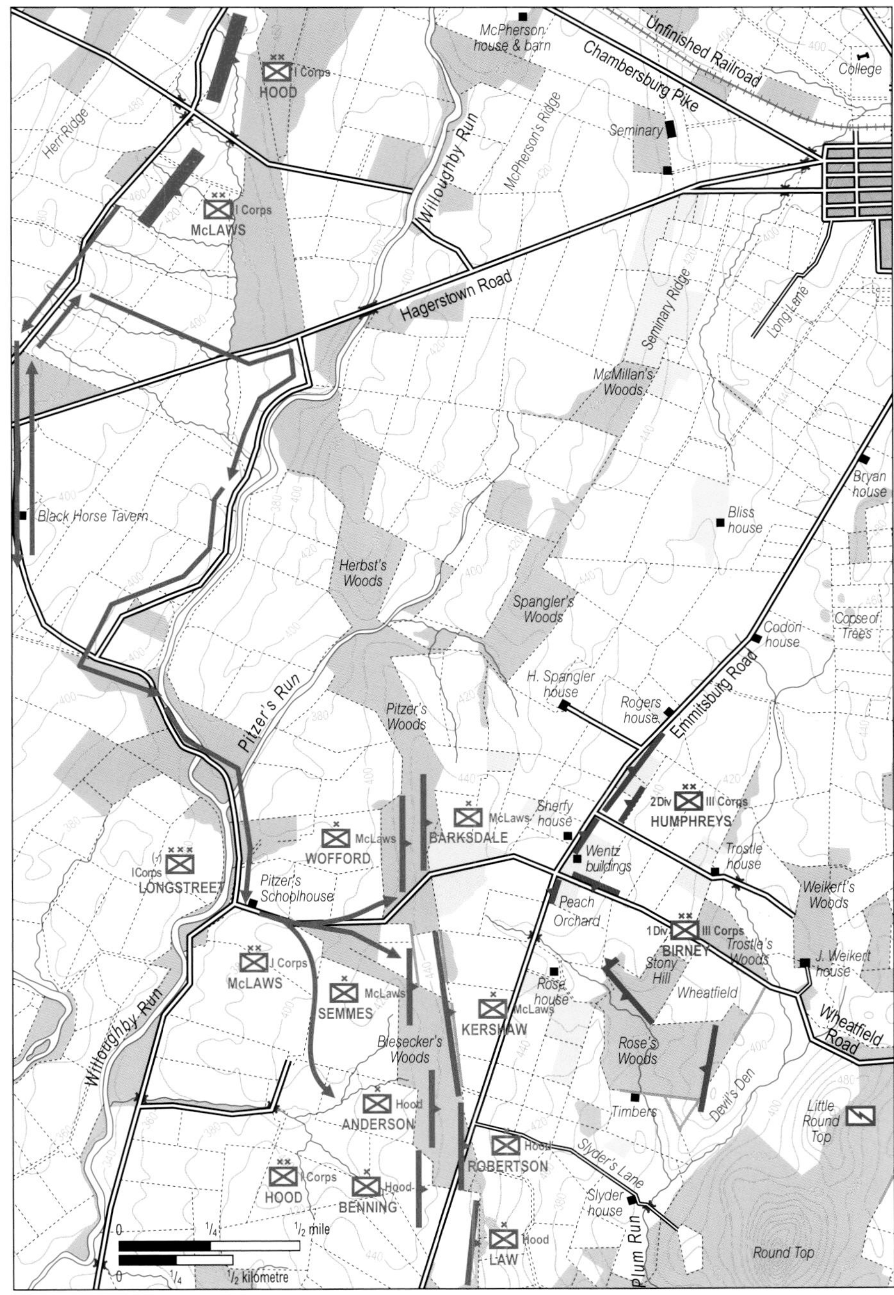

To the great consternation of the Confederates, the Union position was not at all where it had been expected. Instead of conducting an oblique assault perpendicular to the Emmitsburg Road against the Union flank, Longstreet's men would have to make a frontal charge starting from a position parallel to the road. Furthermore, in spite of their efforts to remain undetected, the waiting defenders knew that they were about to be attacked. Longstreet's flank march had been devoid of the type of subordinate initiative that had previously been the hallmark of the Army of Northern Virginia.

1200 hrs	1300	1400	1500	1600	1700	1800	1900	2000	2100	2200
				32-39,67-69	40-43	91-93		70-73		

THE ARMY OF NORTHERN VIRGINIA I CORPS' BATTLES

Hood's Division

Into the Devil's Den – 1600–1730 hrs

Shortly before 1630 hrs, Major-General John Bell Hood rode along his divisional line. He stopped in front of the troops he loved the best, the men of the Texas Brigade. Hood delivered a brief speech. To conclude, he rose in his stirrups, gestured toward the Round Tops, and ordered, 'Fix bayonets, my brave Texans; forward and take those heights!'

The division's right-hand brigade, commanded by Brigadier-General Evander Law, advanced on a line spanning the distance from Round Top to the Devil's Den. Brigadier-General Robertson's Texas Brigade advanced on Law's left. Robertson's orders required him to maintain contact with Law on his right while aligning his left with the Emmitsburg Road. After moving forward only 200 yards, Robertson perceived that this was impossible. Law's men were moving too fast and were also veering away from the road. Accordingly, Robertson resolved to break contact with the road and leave any Federal troops in that area for McLaws to handle. Robertson's left-hand units, the 1st Texas and 3rd Arkansas, moved away from the road and hurried forward to try to align with the brigade's other two regiments. They were unable to do this because those regiments, the 4th and 5th Texas, had maintained their alignment with Law and advanced beyond supporting distance. Thus, the crack Texas Brigade was broken in half even before contact.

Likewise, Law's Brigade became fragmented. As it advanced, it received fire from a Federal battery located on a rise just north of the Devil's Den. While Law's three left-hand regiments continued straight toward Round Top, Law shifted his two right-hand regiments, the 44th and 48th Alabama, to his left flank to deal with this troublesome battery. Consequently, the initial fight at the Devil's Den pitted four Confederate regiments from two different brigades against Ward's Union brigade.

Divisional commander Hood was an able tactician. He probably would have corrected these alignment problems. However, very early in the advance a shell exploded over Hood's head, driving a fragment into his left arm. Hood reeled in his saddle. Aides caught him, lowered him to the ground, and summoned a stretcher. Hood later recalled that as he was carried away he felt, 'deep distress ... at the thought of the inevitable fate of my brave fellow-soldiers, who formed one of the grandest divisions of that world-renown army.' The command passed to Law, with the inevitable associated delays and confusions.

In the front line, the 3rd Arkansas and 1st Texas crossed Plum Run. Having already endured artillery fire from the Peach Orchard, they now encountered musketry from Ward's Brigade. These Federals overlapped the 3rd Arkansas' left flank as that regiment entered Rose's Woods. Colonel Van Manning refused the 3rd's left flank, but this did not leave enough men to oppose successfully a Federal counter-attack moving west through the trees. The 3rd Arkansas retired some 75 yards before this attack. Manning reformed his men in open order and advanced again. This time intense fire forced the regiment to take cover behind trees and rock outcroppings.

Meanwhile, the 1st Texas also met stiff resistance when it tried to advance. It ascended the slope toward the Union battery stationed on the nose of the Devil's Den ridge. The Texans' right flank reached the edge of a stone wall, halted, and opened fire. They were

Longstreet's I Corps should have attacked up the Emmitsburg Road but instead had to align to assault the strong Union forces now beyond the road to the east. After Hood was wounded early in the attack, his division suffered from a loss of tactical control. Law's Brigade manoeuvred particularly erratically.

1200 hrs	1300	1400	1500	1600	1700	1800	1900	2000	2100	2200
pages 30-31				36-39,67-69	40-43	91-93		70-73		

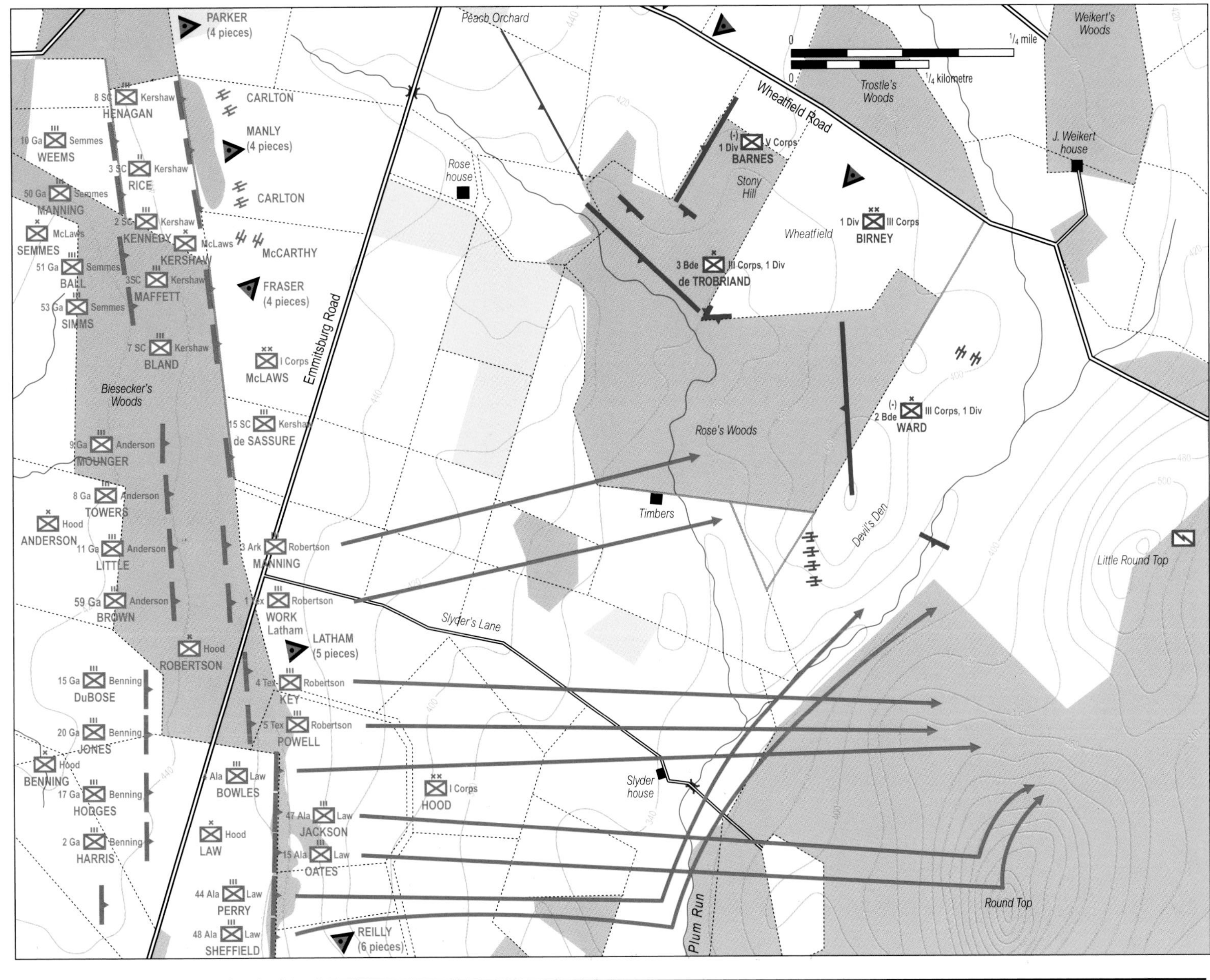

1200 hrs	1300	1400	1500	1600	1700	1800	1900	2000	2100	2200
pages 30-31				36-39,67-69	40-43	91-93		70-73		

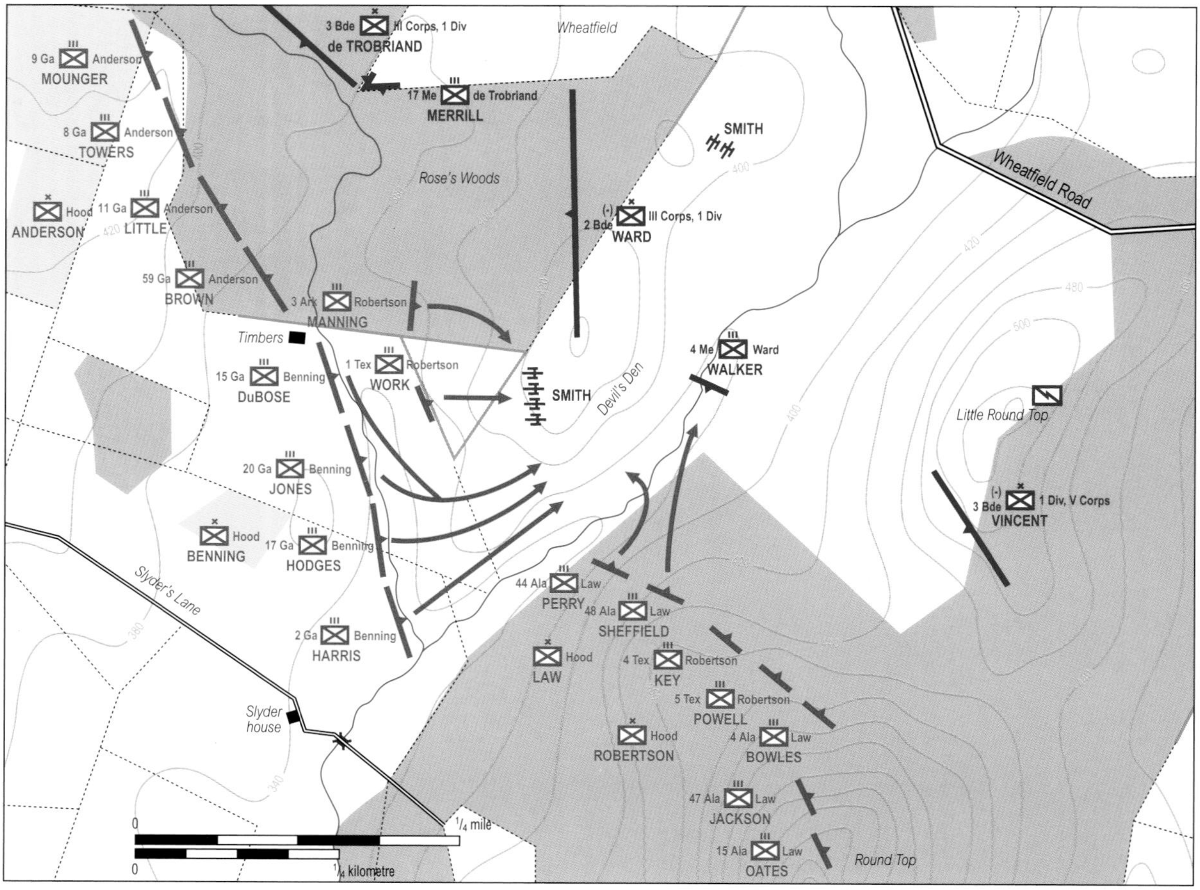

3 Bde III Corps, 1 Div de TROBRIAND
Wheatfield
9 Ga Anderson MOUNGER
17 Me de Trobriand MERRILL
8 Ga Anderson TOWERS
SMITH
Wheatfield Road
Rose's Woods
Hood ANDERSON
11 Ga Anderson LITTLE
(-) 2 Bde III Corps, 1 Div WARD
59 Ga Anderson BROWN
3 Ark Robertson MANNING
Timbers
4 Me Ward WALKER
15 Ga Benning DuBOSE
1 Tex Robertson WORK
SMITH
Devil's Den
Little Round Top
20 Ga Benning JONES
(-) 3 Bde 1 Div, V Corps VINCENT
Hood BENNING
17 Ga Benning HODGES
Slyder's Lane
44 Ala Law PERRY
48 Ala Law SHEFFIELD
2 Ga Benning HARRIS
Hood LAW
4 Tex Robertson KEY
5 Tex Robertson POWELL
Slyder house
Hood ROBERTSON
4 Ala Law BOWLES
47 Ala Law JACKSON
15 Ala Law OATES
Round Top
0 1/4 mile
0 1/4 kilometre

The battle to dislodge the defenders of the Devil's Den, who were ably supported by artillery on the ridge, tied down half of Robertson's brigade and part of Law's command before Benning punched through the centre.

behind the southwestern side of a three-acre, triangular, open field bordered on all sides by stone walls. The wall provided shelter from the Union battery.

A back and forth struggle ensued. Neither Union nor Confederate soldier could survive for long in the open field. In between charge and counter-charge, the opponents settled behind the stone walls and traded volleys. So far, the two Texas Brigade regiments had been outnumbered by their foes. Fortunately, help was at hand.

The two Alabama regiments that Law had moved to his left flank emerged from the woods on the slope of Round Top and found themselves facing the high ground on which sat the Union battery. If they captured this position they would be on the flank of Ward's Union Brigade and would also open a route for an

Benning's Confederates, with units from Law's Brigade, finally take the Devil's Den. (MARS)

1200 hrs	1300	1400	1500	1600	1700	1800	1900	2000	2100	2200
pages 30-31				36-39,67-69	40-43	91-93		70-73		

advance west onto Little Round Top. Law ordered the 44th to capture the battery that blocked the 1st Texas. As the 44th moved through the Devil's Den – the terrible 'cliffs of rocks', recalled one Alabama soldier – a deadly volley from a mass of concealed Union skirmishers inflicted heavy losses. The 44th went to ground. The 48th Alabama, advancing on the right flank of the 44th, tried to push up the Plum Run Gorge. Here it encountered the 4th Maine, which had been positioned along the floor of the ravine. The enemy's stout resistance stalled the rebel advance.

The first Confederate thrust at the Devil's Den became a series of static, but costly, close range fire-fights. The best remembered soldier during this engagement was Texas Private Wilson Barbee. He clambered onto a huge boulder and began firing at the nearby yankees. Wounded soldiers who were sheltered behind the boulder, handed him loaded muskets. Barbee fired 25 times. His prominent position attracted return fire. A ball hit his right leg, knocking him to the ground. He crawled back to his perch until another ball hit his left leg. Returning yet again, Barbee maintained his post until a third ball struck his body. He lay on the ground, cursing his comrades for their failure to lift him back into position to continue the combat.

The fighting continued until Brigadier-General Henry Benning's Georgia Brigade reached the front. Benning had observed that the rebel forces in front of the Devil's Den were weak. He oriented his brigade on the gap between the 1st Texas and Law's 44th Alabama and charged. His charge reinvigorated all of the Confederates in this sector. Someone in the 44th Alabama cried out, 'There is Benning; we are all right now.'

Indeed, the frontal pressure from Benning's Brigade and Robertson's two regiments, combined with Law's renewed flank attack, secured the Devil's Den itself. The 1st Texas and 20th Georgia captured three of the four artillery pieces on the rise overlooking Devil's Den. Indicative of the tenacious Union resistance is the report that the 20th's flag received 87 holes from infantry and artillery fire.

The rebel onslaught carried on over the high ground north of the Devil's Den and into the Plum Run Valley. Colour bearers from the 1st Texas and 15th Georgia vied with one another to position their flags nearest the enemy. When an exploding shell splintered the Texan's flagstaff and blinded him in one eye, the enraged colour bearer tried to charge the yankee line armed with his broken flagstaff! Fortunately, his comrades restrained him. The Confederates continued to take artillery fire. Among the killed on this portion of the field was Colonel John Jones of the 20th Georgia, whose head was blown open by a shell fragment.

The effort to drive the yankees across Plum Run cost the Confederates heavy losses.
(Library of Congress)

A Union counter-attack drove the Confederates from the heights of Devil's Den Ridge. They retired in good order to the cover of the Devil's Den and the nearby woods. The ferocious fighting in the open, rocky area east of the Den and Plum Run gave it the terrible name, the Slaughter Pen.

The Union soldiers were fought out. With the arrival of Benning's Brigade, the Confederates had more and fresher soldiers. Moreover, the yankees knew that their position had been turned on both flanks. One more concerted Confederate advance drove them from the Devil's Den and the adjacent high ground.

A Texas soldier described the action at the Devil's Den as 'one of the wildest, fiercest struggles of the war.' In reality, it featured the type of hard fighting in rough terrain that characterised Civil War combat. Both sides had fought with great determination. But Hood's untimely wounding resulted in the rebels manoeuvering without good tactical coordination. Consequently, they had suffered serious losses. The significance of their sacrifice depended upon the outcome of the fighting on either side of the Devil's Den, most particularly upon the struggle for Little Round Top.

1200 hrs	1300	1400	1500	1600	1700	1800	1900	2000	2100	2200
pages 30-31				36-39,67-69	40-43	91-93		70-73		

THE ARMY OF NORTHERN VIRGINIA I CORPS' BATTLES

Hood's Division

Decision on Little Round Top – 1600–2000 hrs

Little Round Top was a formidable defensive bastion that secured the Army of the Potomac's left flank. If the Confederates captured this hill, the Union position on Cemetery Ridge would become untenable. The Confederate soldiers who attacked Little Round Top knew that they confronted a tough defensive position. The slopes up which the rebels climbed were strewn with rocks and boulders. Several rough lines of rock ledges and shelves provided cover for the defenders.

In 1863, only a few scraggy trees grew along the slopes. However, the attackers would be sheltered from hostile fire until they emerged from the woods on Round Top. In addition, the Union battery on Little Round Top did not enjoy a good field of fire. Likewise, the attackers would be without artillery support. The struggle for the high ground was largely an all-infantry battle.

The intermingling of regiments belonging to Robertson and Law that occurred during the approach to the Devil's Den influenced the Confederate charge on Little Round Top. Three regiments – Robertson's 4th and 5th Texas and Law's 4th Alabama – crossed Plum Run, wheeled left into the woods on the northwest slope of Round Top, and encountered yankee sharpshooters behind a wall as they advanced against Little Round Top. Meanwhile, Law's 47th and 15th Alabama first climbed up Round Top and then descended to attack the left flank of the Federal brigade defending Little Round Top.

The sharpshooters' careful fire killed an officer in the 4th Texas and wounded both its colonel and lieutenant-colonel. Thus before the attack was truly underway, Major John Bane found himself in command of the regiment. The Texas infantry cleared the wall of enemy marksmen. Then Colonel Robert Powell of the 5th Texas ordered his men forward with the 4th Texas and 4th Alabama conforming to this advance on Powell's left and right, respectively. The men climbed some 400 yards, passing over and around 'large boulders, from the size of a wash pot to that of a wagon bed.' To their left they could see the struggle in the area of the Devil's Den. To their right, concealed by the trees, were the 47th and 15th Alabama.

Colonel William Oates had overall command of both regiments. General Law had instructed Oates to wheel left after crossing Plum Run and thus extend the line advancing against Little Round Top. However, some yankee sharpshooters retired up the slope of Round Top after firing at Oates' Alabamians. Oates was a free-thinking officer who often found literal subordination difficult. He concluded that he could not leave enemy troops on his left and rear and so

The hasty works on the commanding heights of Little Round Top were erected after the epic defence by Weed's and Vincent's Union brigades on July 2. (U.S. National Archives)

1200 hrs	1300	1400	1500	1600	1700	1800	1900	2000	2100	2200
pages 30-31				32-35,67-69	40-43	91-93		70-73		

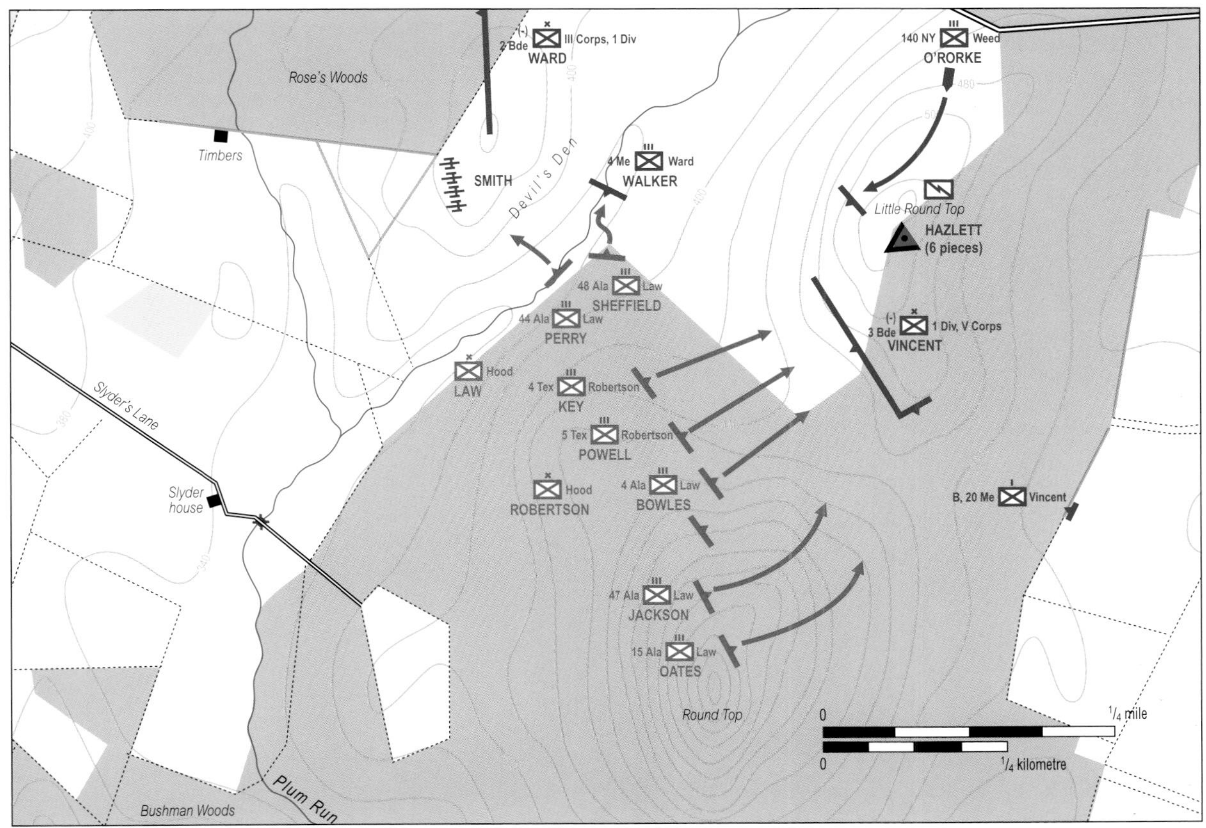

The unplanned climb of Round Top by the two regiments of Law's brigade, under Colonel Oates, critically reduced the number of troops available for the initial charge against Little Round Top by Robertson's men.

disobeyed orders and headed due east up Round Top.

Both regiments gained the crest without meeting any opposition. Here they paused. They were exhausted after the long march from New Guilford and from the steep ascent on a hot July day. Furthermore, the 22 men who had been sent off with canteens to procure water had not returned, so they were thirsty as well.

At this juncture, one of Law's staff officers arrived. He told Oates that there were no Union troops on Oates' left and reminded him that Hood's orders were to capture Little Round Top without delay. Oates protested. Then and thereafter he believed that he held the field's dominant high ground. He later wrote that within 30 minutes he could convert his position into a Gibraltar-like fortress and defend it against all comers. This was ridiculous because his division was on the attack, not the defensive. The staff officer insisted that Oates rejoin the attack against Little Round Top. Reluctantly, the colonel acceded.

Meanwhile, the three other regiments entered the open terrain at the foot of Little Round Top. Here they could see that they confronted a defended position. In fact, some 1,000 Union troops stood poised in position to resist them. The rebels laboriously clambered up the boulder-strewn slope. The first volleys killed Colonel Powell of the 5th Texas and seriously wounded the unit's lieutenant-colonel. Colonel Scruggs of the 4th Alabama reported, 'We advanced up the mountain under a galling fire'. The attacking rebels perceived that they carried the yankees' first line, advanced another 200 yards, and then met a second 'fortified' line. In fact, they confronted a battle line sheltered behind rocks and boulders. The destructive fire from this line caused all three regiments to recoil.

After a brief rest, their officers rallied them and they charged again. The command of the 5th Texas had

1200 hrs	1300	1400	1500	1600	1700	1800	1900	2000	2100	2200
pages 30-31				32-35,67-69	40-43	91-93		70-73		

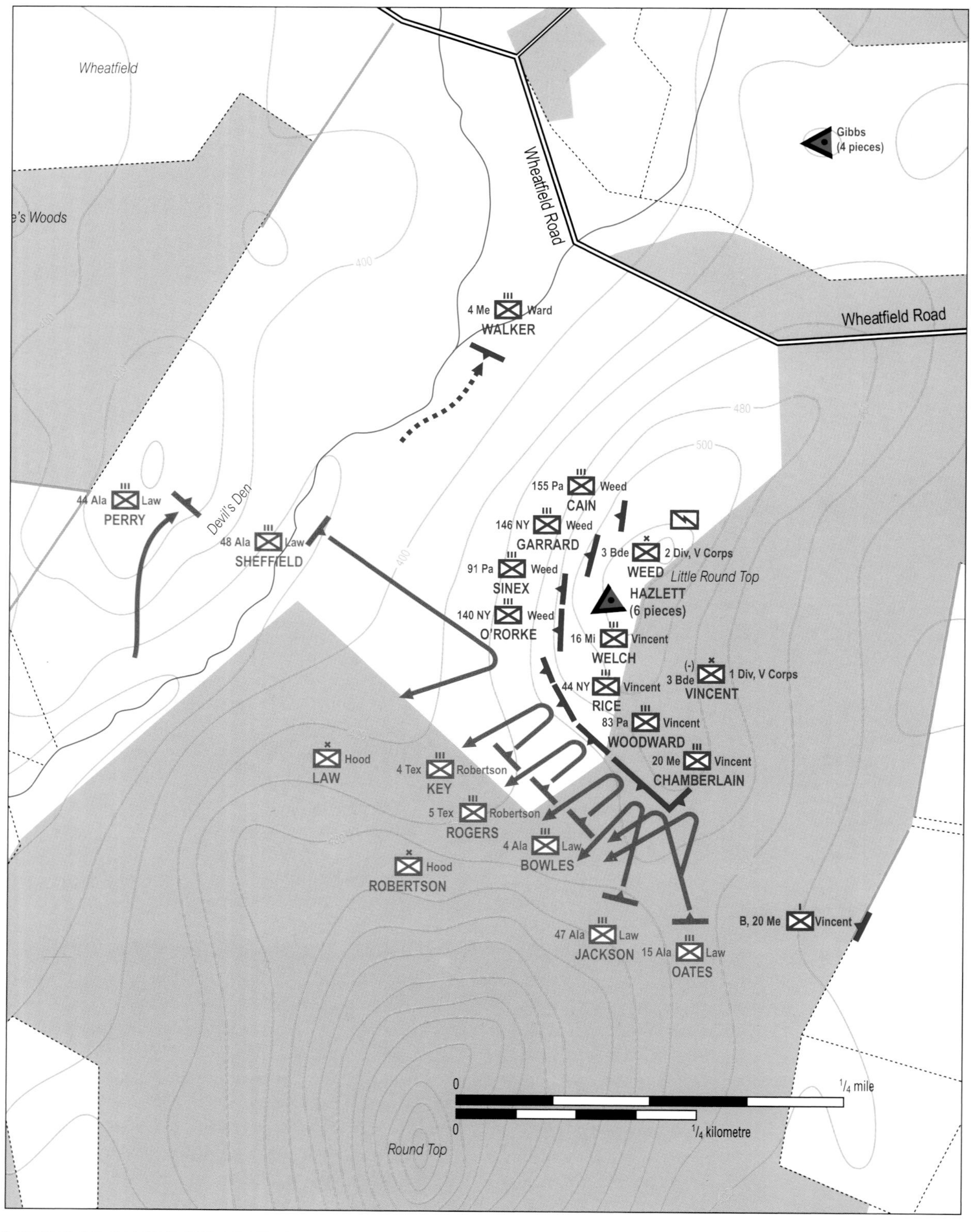

1200 hrs	1300	1400	1500	1600	1700	1800	1900	2000	2100	2200
pages 30-31				32-35,67-69	40-43	91-93		70-73		

***Left:* The subsequent assault against Little Round Top confronted better prepared defenders occupying a naturally strong position.**

devolved upon Major Rogers. He reported that his men 'advanced boldly over the ground strewn with the bodies of their dead and dying comrades to the base of what they knew to be an impregnable fortification.' Again the charge failed. When Rogers counted noses, he found that nearly two-thirds of the regiment were dead or wounded.

Then Oates' men entered the fray. They too encountered heavy fire, 'the most destructive fire I ever saw' recalled Oates. Repulsed, they, like the other Confederates, sought cover. A prolonged and costly fire-fight ensued. At last the surviving officers managed to form the battered regiments into a line of battle and the Confederates charged uphill again. This was the third charge by the three left-hand regiments of the brigade. The hostile fire had not slackened. Some of their efforts lacked conviction.

Yet their opponents were nearly fought out as well. Better still, the 48th Alabama, having completed its actions at the Devil's Den, arrived to bolster the Confederate left. Emboldened, soldiers courageously climbed nearly to the summit only to be repelled by Union reinforcements. Some rebels ran the gauntlet to safety. Others raised their hands in surrender.

At about the same time, Oates' men tried to work their way around the Federal left flank. Oates hoped to be able to enfilade the yankee position and thus capture the heights. The 15th Alabama advanced, only to encounter again a terrible fire. They 'wavered like a man trying to walk into a strong wind.' Among the Confederate casualties was Oates' brother who had rallied from his sick bed to join his men.

The issue hung in the balance. The fighting was at such close quarters that Colonel Oates himself fired his pistol at 10-foot range when a yankee tried to capture the colours of the 15th Alabama. The Union commander well described the scene: 'The edge of the fight rolled backward and forward like a wave.' When the Union defenders launched a do or die counter-attack, the Confederates could not withstand it. Oates ordered a retreat. A survivor recalls, 'when the signal was given we ran like a herd of wild cattle.'

The five regiments rallied in the shelter of the Devil's Den. They had fought manfully, suffered fearful losses, and failed. Incomplete returns suggest the scale of their losses. The 4th Alabama, 15th Alabama and 47th Alabama lost 87, 161, and 40 officers and men killed, wounded, or missing, respectively. The 4th and 5th Texas lost 87 and 109 men, respectively. One Texas colonel was killed, the other suffered a serious wound.

Although Longstreet's Corps performed prodigies of valour, the effort required great sacrifice. Confederate dead in the Slaughter Pen.
(Library of Congress)

The attackers had confronted a stiff challenge. Hood's wounding at the outset of the advance and Oates' insubordination conspired with difficult terrain defended by determined troops to thwart their gallant attempt. The inability of Hood's men to envelop the Union left and capture Little Round Top meant that if a Confederate breakthrough were to occur, it would have to take place in the Federal centre.

1200 hrs	1300	1400	1500	1600	1700	1800	1900	2000	2100	2200
pages 30-31				32-35,67-69	40-43	91-93		70-73		

THE ARMY OF NORTHERN VIRGINIA I CORPS' BATTLES

McLaws' Division

The Wheatfield and the Peach Orchard – 1700–2000 hrs

The five Georgia regiments commanded by 'Tige' Anderson were the last of Hood's units to engage. They advanced into Rose's Woods to support Robertson's 1st Texas and 3rd Arkansas. Because of the unusual configuration of the Union line, the 59th and 11th Georgia entered the open end of a V-shaped position. Thus they received fire from the front and both flanks. The 11th, in particular, suffered from enfilade fire from a Maine regiment positioned behind a stone wall on the edge of the Wheatfield. The brigade's other regiments crossed a branch of Plum Run and encountered stiff resistance from the yankees at the base of Stony Hill. After a 30 to 40 minute combat, the brigade fell back to its start line.

The charge had failed in large part because it received no support from McLaws' men. Anderson coordinated his next effort with the colonel of the nearest regiment in Kershaw's South Carolina Brigade. While walking his line to prepare a second charge, Anderson received a disabling wound. Lieutenant-Colonel Luffman assumed brigade command.

Meanwhile, a three-shot cannon salvo signalled the start of McLaws' attack. Side by side, Anderson's and Kershaw's brigades charged at about 1700 hrs. Semmes' Brigade followed Kershaw in support. From the edge of Biesecker's Woods, Cabell's Artillery Battalion provided support. It was the most coordinated charge by any of Longstreet's units so far.

Kershaw intended to cross the Emmitsburg Road, wheel to his left, and join Hood's men in a drive against the Union flank. The South Carolinians advanced 'with the precision of a brigade drill' through a terrible artillery fire from at least 30 guns in the Peach Orchard and along the Wheatfield Road. The regiments began to crowd together. Kershaw sent orders to adjust the line. Several regiments complied. However, those on the brigade's left misunderstood. Having arrived within point-blank range of the batteries on the Wheatfield Road, when success seemed certain, someone ordered them to wheel to their right. This exposed their flank to the guns and caused heavy losses. Kershaw related, 'hundreds of the bravest and best men of Carolina fell, victims of this fatal blunder.'

While these unfortunate regiments rallied, Anderson's Brigade and Kershaw's right-hand regiments attacked Stony Hill and the Wheatfield. Here a Union mistake removed supporting troops at a key time. The rebels captured the high ground and entered the Wheatfield. This occurred about the same time that Hood's men cleared the Devil's Den. After repelling a brave but doomed Federal counter-attack, it seemed like the Confederates had finally gained the enemy flank. Anderson's Brigade controlled Rose's Woods with support from the 1st Texas and 15th Georgia and Kershaw held Stony Hill.

Before the Confederates could exploit their situation, a ferocious division-sized counter-attack came screaming out of Trostle's Woods and into the Wheatfield. Kershaw said of the 7th South Carolina, 'These men were brave veterans who had fought from Bull Run to Gettysburg and knew the strength of their position, and held it as long as it was tenable.' Eventually, the yankees drove the Confederates across Plum Run and reclaimed the Wheatfield and Stony Hill. Except for the Devil's Den, the original Union line was restored.

While Kershaw's men rallied around the Rose Farm, they saw Wofford's Brigade 'coming in in splendid style.' Wofford's men marched astride the Wheatfield Road on Kershaw's left. Semmes' Brigade added support on Kershaw's opposite flank. Kershaw again attacked Stony Hill. Anderson's Brigade, making its third major assault, charged the south side of the Wheatfield. Thus four Confederate brigades

1200 hrs	1300	1400	1500	1600	1700	1800	1900	2000	2100	2200
pages 30-31				32-39,67-69		91-93		70-73		

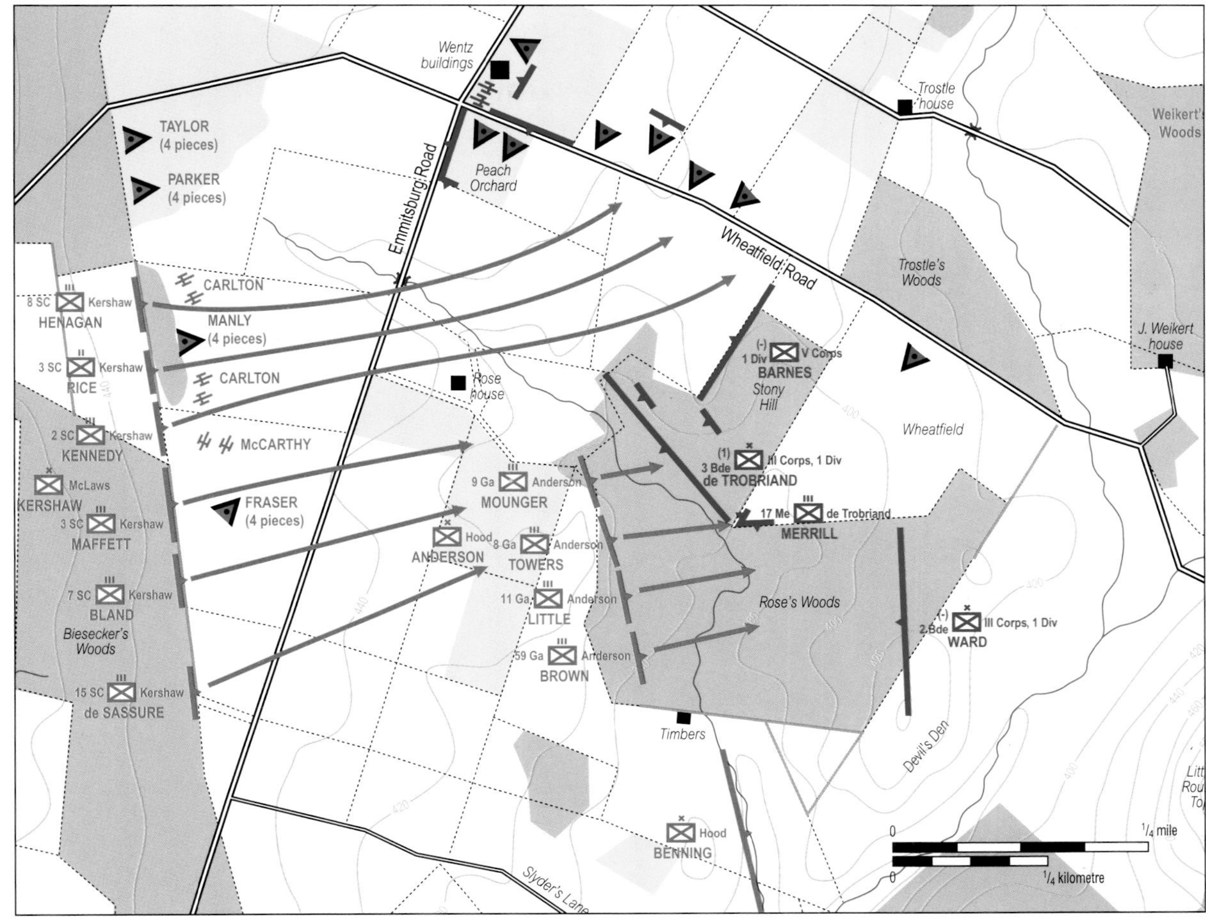

Kershaw's Brigade assaults Stony Hill and charges the Union gun line to the north of the Wheatfield Road.

converged on the field. They sent the Federal forces reeling. When Wofford cleared Trostle's Woods, there were no remaining Union units west of Plum Run on this part of the battlefield. In a disjointed series of ferocious charges, seven rebel brigades had shattered ten Federal brigades.

About the time that the Union counter-attack had reclaimed the Wheatfield, McLaws began his attack on the Peach Orchard. McLaws' mission was to take the high ground around the Peach Orchard and alongside Hood, roll up the Union left flank. Initially, McLaws had formed his brigades astride the Wheatfield Road opposite the Peach Orchard. Cabell's Artillery Battalion deployed in front of the division's right flank. Four more batteries belonging to Alexander's Battalion deployed in front of McLaws' centre.

Hood's inability to drive the yankees from the Wheatfield compelled McLaws to commit all of Semmes' and some of Kershaw's brigades to support Hood. Thus, Kershaw's left wing and Barksdale's Brigade were left to spearhead the attack on the Peach Orchard with Wofford's Brigade in support.

The effort began with a prolonged artillery duel. The range to the target was 700 to 800 yards, so even the Confederate 12-pounder howitzers could usefully contribute. But the Union line also had numerous batteries. Illustrative of the deadly nature of this fire was the fate of Captain John Fraser's Pulaski Artillery. After a 60-minute exchange of fire, Federal shells had mortally wounded Fraser and inflicted severe losses. His replacement had to consolidate the survivors to crew a two-gun section. The other pieces remained silent. Moody's Louisiana battery needed reinforce-

1200 hrs	1300	1400	1500	1600	1700	1800	1900	2000	2100	2200
pages 30-31				32-39,67-69		91-93		70-73		

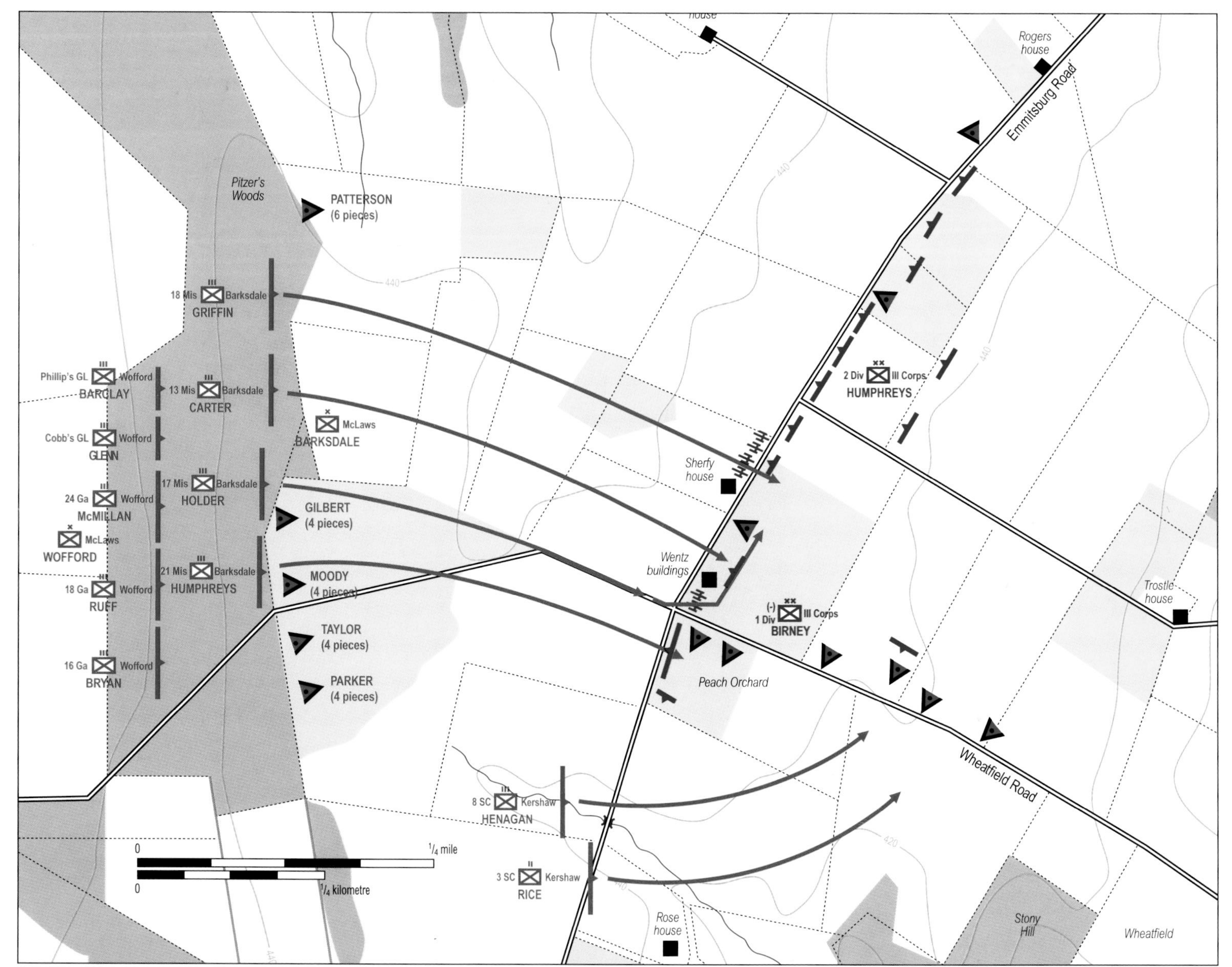

1200 hrs	1300	1400	1500	1600	1700	1800	1900	2000	2100	2200
pages 30-31				32-39,67-69		91-93		70-73		

In a gallant charge, Barksdales' Mississippians broke through the Federal defence at the Peach Orchard.

ments from Barksdale's infantry. By the end of the action, five of eight volunteers were either dead or wounded. Although the rebel artillery inflicted serious losses on the defenders' line, by the time the infantry charged there was a solid rank of Union artillery to oppose them consisting of 40 pieces extending from the Sherfy House to the Peach Orchard and east along the Wheatfield Road to Stony Hill.

The excitable Brigadier-General William Barksdale had chafed while his brigade was under bombardment. He said to Longstreet, 'I wish you would let me go in, General; I would take that battery in five minutes.' Longstreet replied, 'Wait a little, we are all going in presently.'

Somehow when the moment came, Barksdale was tardy. Kershaw and Semmes' brigades had already advanced, received the undivided attention of the Federal gun line around Stony Hill, and been repulsed. However, when the Mississippians did advance, they charged with tremendous spirit. Orders dictated that the regimental officers leave their horses to the rear. Thus, the mounted Barksdale made a prominent display when he rode in front of his old regiment, the 13th Mississippi, and shouted: 'Attention, Mississippians! Battalions, Forward!'

Barksdale's regiments converged on a 350-yard long front extending from the Peach Orchard to the Sherfy House. The Confederate artillery fire had depleted the Union batteries and unsettled the infantry. The Mississippians crashed through the apex of the Union line at the intersection of the Emmitsburg Road and the Wheatfield Road. They turned to their left to flank the adjacent yankee units. Meanwhile, Wofford's Brigade passed Barksdale's left flank. As noted earlier, their presence stiffened the resolve of Kershaw's men and contributed to the eventual rebel success in the Wheatfield.

When Barksdale broke through the crust of the defence at the Peach Orchard, he placed the nearby Federal units in a poor tactical position. The rebels could now flank the Union troops along the Wheatfield Road and charge into the left rear of the forces along the Emmitsburg Road. One by one the yankee units dissolved until the entire line broke to the rear.

Barksdale had redeemed his pledge 'to take that battery in five minutes.' As Barksdale's Brigade continued its advance, it eventually reached the line of Plum Run. Here it appeared that at last the Confederate battle plan was on the verge of success. If Anderson's Division supported Barksdale vigorously, the Union centre stood imperilled.

Longstreet's two divisions each lost about 30 per cent of their men. Longstreet would proudly refer to his corps' fighting on this day as 'the best three hours' fighting ever done by any troops on any battlefield.'

Carnage at the Trostle house by the Peach Orchard, with dead horses from the 9th Massachusetts Artillery. (Library of Congress)

1200 hrs	1300	1400	1500	1600	1700	1800	1900	2000	2100	2200
pages 30-31				32-39,67-69		91-93		70-73		

THE ARMY OF NORTHERN VIRGINIA

II CORPS

July 1 had not been a brilliant day for Lieutenant-General Richard Ewell. He would later candidly say that it took a number of blunders to lose the Battle of Gettysburg and that he had committed his share. He had exerted little influence over the combat and a negative restraint during the pursuit phase. He successfully persuaded Lee to let him hold his position and promised to attack on the morning of July 2.

Two of the corps' divisions had engaged on July 1. They incurred significant losses. A total of 3,472 men had been killed, wounded, or missing. The losses were unequally distributed. Rodes' Division suffered particularly heavily, with Iverson's Brigade losing 60% of its strength and Daniel's 37%. Early's Division, by virtue of its fortuitous arrival on the Union flank, fared much better. Johnson's Division had arrived late in the day and did not engage. As a result, Ewell commanded a mixed group with Rodes much battered, Johnson fresh, and Early's men somewhat depleted but in good spirits having driven the enemy the day before.

The corps' final tactical position at the end of the first day was exceedingly poor. The Union strong point on Cemetery Hill compelled the corps to operate along exterior lines. Johnson's Division faced Culp's Hill. Early's Division sought shelter in the southwestern suburbs of Gettysburg and confronted Cemetery Hill. Rodes' Division lay scattered from the middle of town west to Seminary Ridge. There were no convenient lateral communications to permit the shifting of forces from one division to another. In the vernacular of the day, each would fight 'on its own hook.' Two-thirds of the corps, Johnson and Early, were virtually out of supporting range of the remainder of the army. Also troubling was the corps' unsecured left flank and rear. Both Johnson and Early felt the need to detach a brigade to provide flank security. The corps also confronted some of the most difficult terrain on the entire field. Later it could be seen more plainly – Culp's Hill was virtually an impregnable citadel, Cemetery Hill an artillery fortress.

Ewell's original plan had been to occupy Culp's Hill. He had received a scout's report that this vital position was unoccupied. When he learned otherwise, he

II CORPS

Lieutenant-General Richard Stoddert Ewell

17 Staff and Field Officers

Early's Division
Major-General Jubal Anderson Early
Johnson's Division
Major-General Edward Johnson
Rodes' Division
Major-General Robert Emmett Rodes
II Corps Reserve Artillery
Colonel John Thompson Brown

II CORPS HEADQUARTERS

PROVOST GUARD & ESCORT
Cos A & B, 1st Battalion North Carolina Sharpshooters
Major Rufus Watson Wharton
57 troops present for duty equipped
Co. B, 39th Battalion Virginia Cavalry
Captain William F. Randolph

Lieutenant-General Richard Stoddert Ewell received criticism for his lack of initiative at Gettysburg. He later admitted, 'it took a dozen blunders to lose Gettysburg and I committed a good many of them.' (Carl Smith, Manassas)

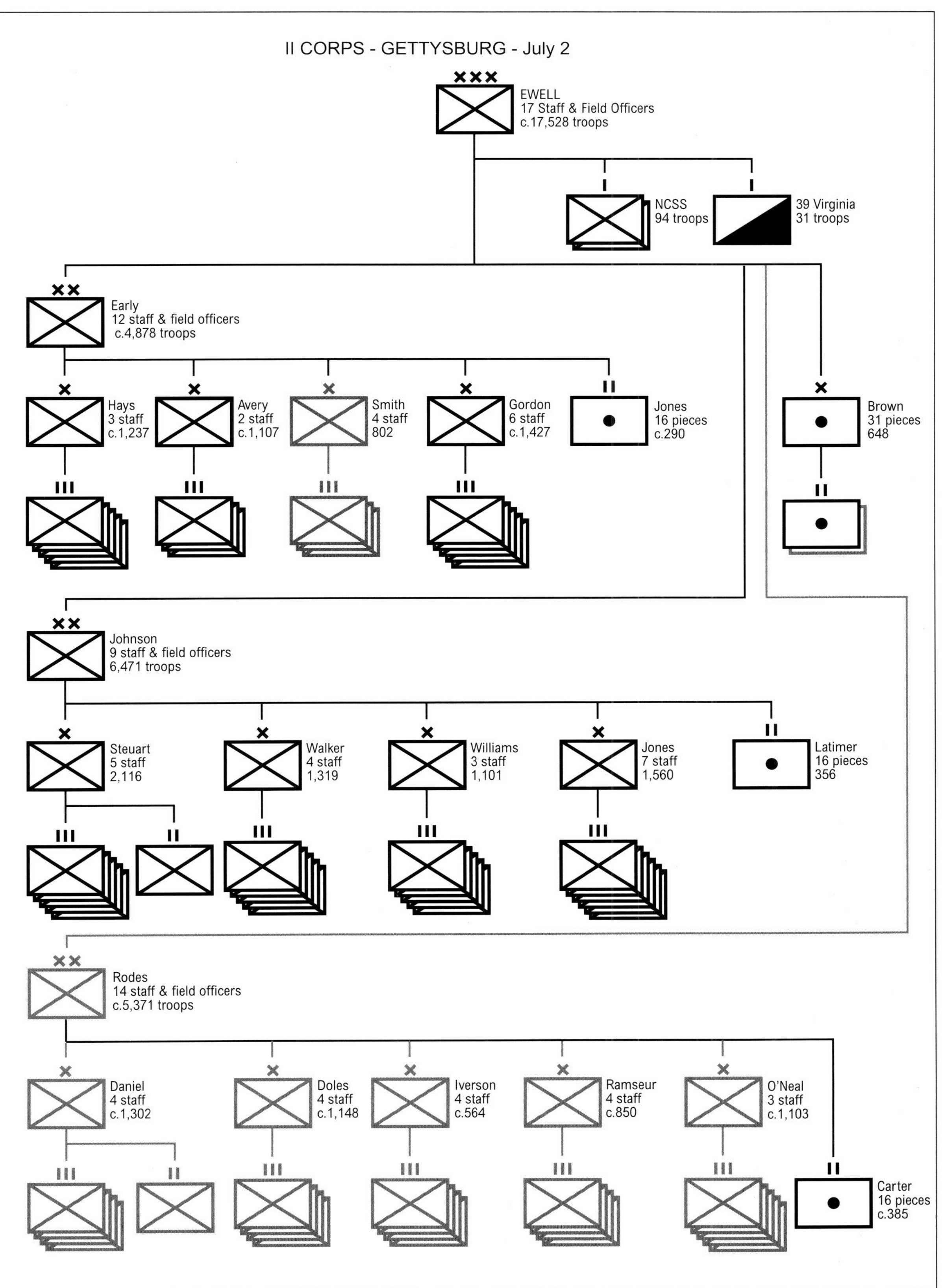
II CORPS - GETTYSBURG - July 2
EWELL
17 Staff & Field Officers
c.17,528 troops
NCSS
94 troops
39 Virginia
31 troops
Early
12 staff & field officers
c.4,878 troops
Hays
3 staff
c.1,237
Avery
2 staff
c.1,107
Smith
4 staff
802
Gordon
6 staff
c.1,427
Jones
16 pieces
c.290
Brown
31 pieces
648
Johnson
9 staff & field officers
6,471 troops
Steuart
5 staff
2,116
Walker
4 staff
1,319
Williams
3 staff
1,101
Jones
7 staff
1,560
Latimer
16 pieces
356
Rodes
14 staff & field officers
c.5,371 troops
Daniel
4 staff
c.1,302
Doles
4 staff
c.1,148
Iverson
4 staff
c.564
Ramseur
4 staff
c.850
O'Neal
3 staff
c.1,103
Carter
16 pieces
c.385

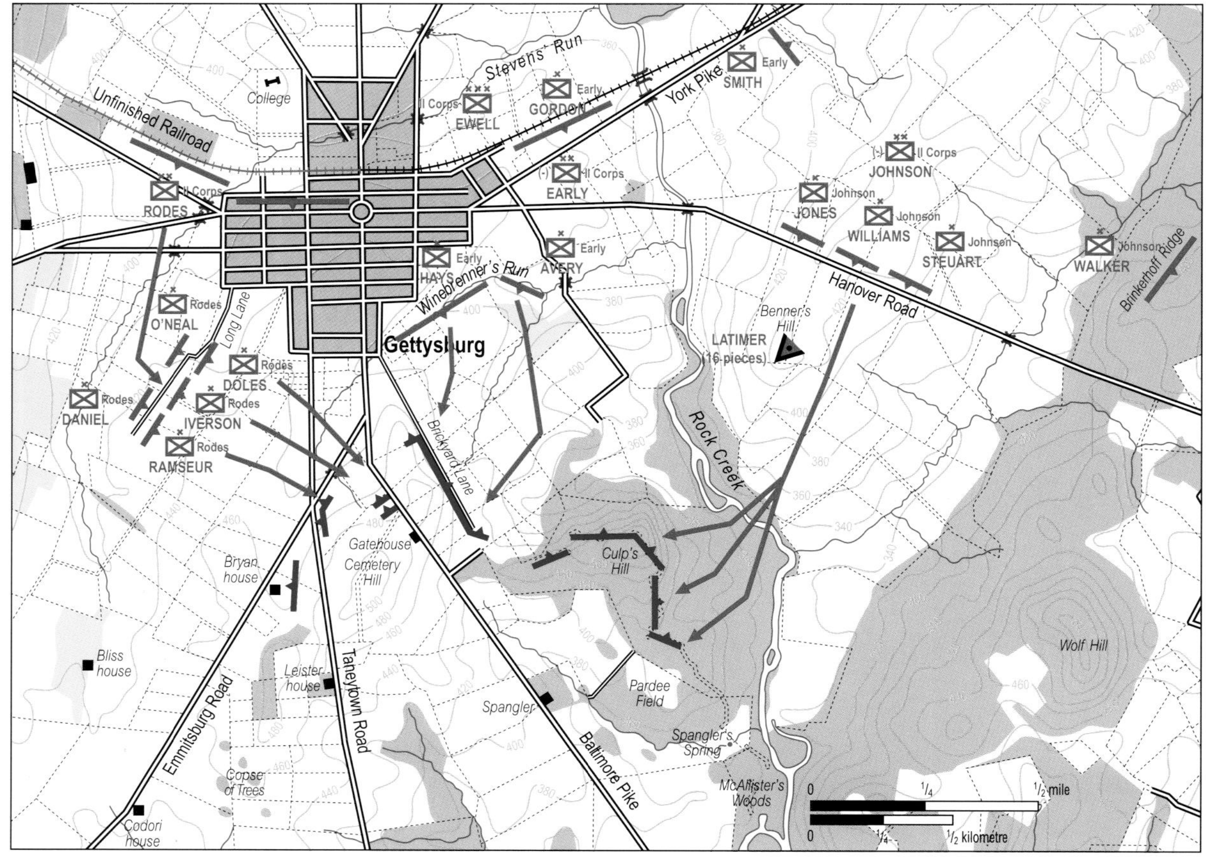

II Corps was to demonstrate against the Federal right flank in support of Longstreet's attack on the Union left. Johnson's and Early's advances, against Culp's and Cemetery Hills respectively, turned into full assaults. Rodes was to deploy west of Cemetery Hill to support Early but failed to advance beyond Long Lane.

cancelled Johnson's assault and waited to harmonise his corps' operations with the rest of Lee's army. He knew that Lee wanted him to create a diversion in favour of Longstreet. Accordingly, he stayed up most of the night to ensure that Johnson's Division and the brigades of Hays and Hoke (Avery) were ready to advance when they heard Longstreet's guns.

Shortly after dawn, Major Venable of Lee's staff arrived to inquire again if Ewell thought he could make a breakthrough on his corps' front. Ewell conducted Venable on an extensive tour of his positions. They could see that the yankees had availed themselves of the nocturnal hours to pack Cemetery Hill with artillery.

The Union infantry appeared to have recovered and was manning stout-appearing lines behind stone walls and breastworks. Ewell was devoid of any ideas about how to tackle this formidable position.

In turn, Lee's initial plan, which was to begin the Confederate attack on the morning of July 2, had to be modified when Longstreet failed to get his men in position on time. Lee met with Ewell some time around 0900 hrs in the cupola of the Adams County almshouse. From this vantage they could see the formidable defences opposing Ewell. Lee postponed Ewell's attack until Longstreet was ready. This delay led to many soldiers engaging in a costly skirmish before the attack order came. While the skirmishers fought their deadly little duels, the remainder of the corps waited, contemplating their likely fate against an enemy's position that was growing stronger before their eyes. Finally, around 1600 hrs, the corps' artillery opened its preparatory bombardment.

II Corps Casualties at Gettysburg July 2 1863

Infantry killed or wounded 1,180
Infantry missing/captured 350
Artillery killed or wounded 77
Artillery missing/captured 0

II Corps – Early's Division

The first of July had been a shining day for Early's Division. It began by marching to the sound of the guns. Arriving about one mile north of Gettysburg, Major-General Jubal Early saw the Federal XI Corps deploying to engage Rodes' Division. Early committed three brigades into an impetuous assault that struck XI Corps' right flank on Blocher's Knoll. The Confederates routed their foe, inflicting hundreds of losses. Early's men pursued the yankees into Gettysburg but came up short against Cemetery Hill. The division lost 101 men killed, 433 wounded, and 54 missing. It probably inflicted about three times more casualties on the enemy force.

Lee, Ewell and Early conducted a back and forth debate about how to proceed during the evening of July 1 and on into the morning of the next day. As the battle plan finally materialised, Early's Division received the assignment of making a diversionary attack against Cemetery Hill in conjunction with Rodes' Division. The attack was to begin after Johnson's Division charged against Culp's Hill.

EARLY'S DIVISION
Major-General Jubal Anderson Early

Hays' Brigade - c.1,237 troops
Hoke's (Avery's) Brigade - c.1,107 troops
Smith's Brigade - 802 troops
Gordon's Brigade - c.1,427 troops
Jones' Artillery Battalion - 281 troops

Major-General Jubal Anderson Early and his division performed brilliantly on July 1. The next day they confronted an imposing defensive bastion on Cemetery Hill. (Carl Smith, Manassas)

Early had Hays' and Avery's Brigades in position southeast of Gettysburg and ready to attack. Around midday he recalled Gordon's Brigade from the York Pike, where it had been providing flank security, and moved it behind the two assault brigades. He left the Stonewall Brigade on the York Pike along Brinkerhoff's Ridge to maintain its guard of the army's flank.

During the day the waiting rebels could see the Union forces continue to dig in on the crest and slope of Cemetery Hill.

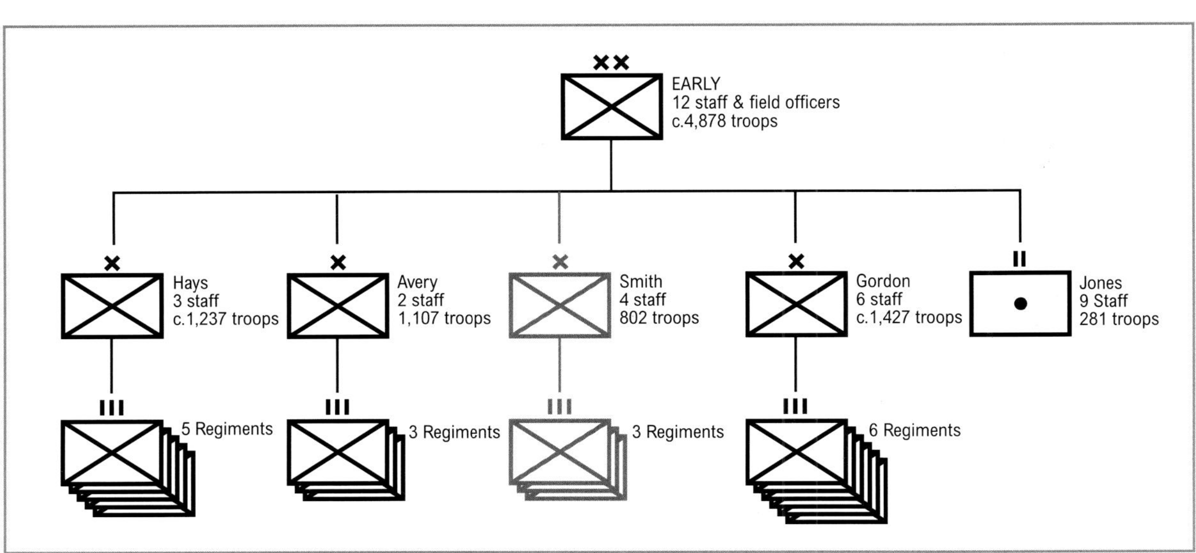

Hays' Brigade

The 1,200 men of Brigadier-General Harry Hays spent a miserable July 2 sheltered in a ravine while waiting to assault Cemetery Hill. The previous day they had participated in the victorious attack against the Federal XI Corps. The brigade had suffered fairly lightly, losing 7 killed, 41 wounded and 15 missing.

Brigadier-General Harry Thompson Hays and his men may have been the first Confederates to enter the town of Gettysburg on the afternoon of July 1. His brigade of Louisianans took many prisoners and suffered few casualties. On July 2, he would assault Cemetery Hill. (USAMHI, Carlisle)

Because the initial plan called for a prompt attack on July 2, the brigade moved into position in the ravine of Winebrenner's Run early in the morning. The ravine was airless and unshaded. As the July sun climbed the soldiers became increasingly uncomfortable. When he learned that the assault was delayed, General Ewell

HAYS' BRIGADE
Brigadier-General Harry Thompson Hays

5th Louisiana Infantry Regiment
Major Alexander Hart/
Captain Thomas H. Biscoe
6th Louisiana Infantry Regiment
Lieutenant-Colonel Joseph Hanlon
7th Louisiana Infantry Regiment
Colonel Davidson Bradfute Penn
8th Louisiana Infantry Regiment
Colonel Trevanion D. Lewis/
Lieutenant-Colonel Alcibiades de Blanc/
Major German Albert Lester
9th Louisiana Infantry Regiment
Colonel Leroy Augustus Stafford

5th Louisiana Infantry Regiment

Co. A	Crescent City Guards
Co. B	Chalmette Rifle Guards
Co. C	Bienville Guards
Co. D	DeSoto Rifles
Co. E	Orleans Cadet Co.
Co. F	Orleans Southrons
Co. G	Louisiana Swamp Rangers
Co. H	Perret Guards
Co. I	Carondelet Invincibles
Co. K	Monroe Guards

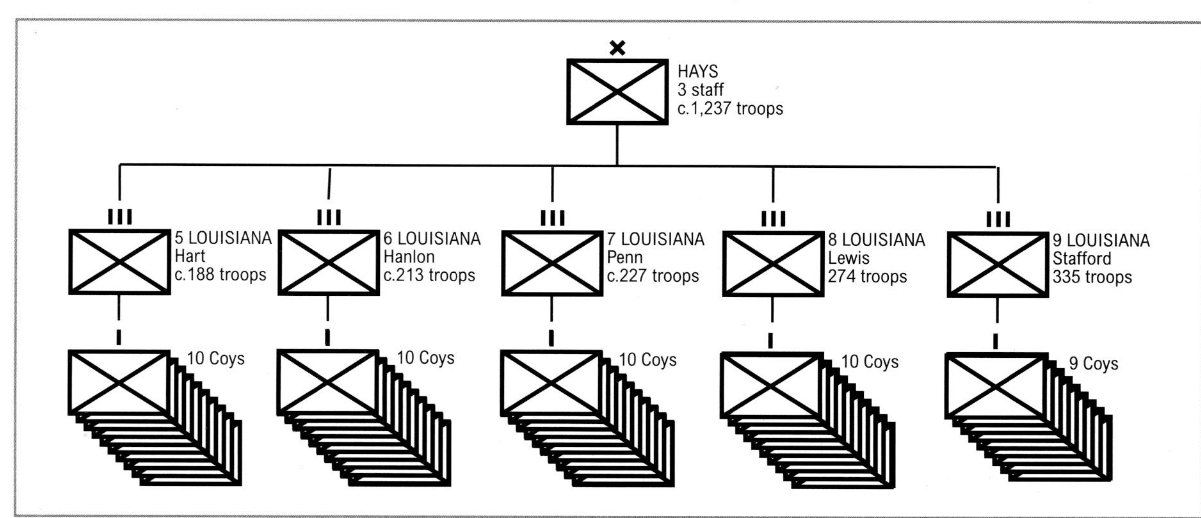

6th Louisiana Infantry Regiment

Co. A	Union and Sabine Guards
Co. B	Calhoun Guards
Co. C	St Landry Light Guards
Co. D	Tensas Rifles
Co. E	Mercer Guards
Co. F	Irish Brigade Co.
Co. G	Pemberton Rangers
Co. H	Orleans Rifles
Co. I	Irish Brigade Co. A
Co. K	Violet Guards

8th Louisiana Infantry Regiment

Co. A	Creole Guards
Co. B	Bienville Rifles
Co. C	Attakapas Guards
Co. D	Sumter Guards
Co. E	Franklin Sharpshooters
Co. F	Opelousas Guards
Co. G	Minden Blues
Co. H	Cheneyville Rifles
Co. I	Rapides Invincibles
Co. K	Phoenix Co.

wanted to pull them back into Gettysburg. However, with Union artillery and sharpshooters present, such a move would result in significant losses.

A prolonged duel between opposing skirmish lines ensued. Company I of the 8th Louisiana was in the front line. An officer stationed with the picket reserve remembers his unit remained pinned behind a fence because 'if anyone showed himself or a hat was seen above the fence a volley was poured into us.' Meanwhile in the ravine, if a man stood upright he risked immediate death from the Federal marksmen.

Overnight Hays' men had heard the Union troops atop Cemetery Hill 'chopping away and working like beavers' as they fortified their position. Daylight confirmed the soldiers' worst fears. Yankee artillerymen had dug in their pieces to create a position 'bristling with a most formidable array of cannon.'

7th Louisiana Infantry Regiment

Co. A	Continental Guards
Co. B	Baton Rouge Fencibles
Co. C	Sarsfield Rangers
Co. D	Virginia Guards
Co. E	Crescent City Rifles Co. B
Co. F	Irish Volunteers
Co. G	American Rifles
Co. H	Crescent City Rifles Co. C
Co. I	Virginia Blues
Co. K	Livingston Rifles

9th Louisiana Infantry Regiment

Co. A	Moore Fencibles
Co. B	Stafford Guides
Co. C	Bienville Blues
Co. D	Bossier Volunteers
Co. E	Milliken Bend Guards
Co. F	DeSoto Blues
Co. G	Colyell Guards
Co. H	Brush Valley Guards
Co. I	Washington Rifles

Hoke's (Avery's) Brigade

In accordance with the initial plan calling for a dawn attack on July 2, Hoke's Brigade, under the command of Colonel Isaac Avery, moved into position in the ravine of Winebrenner's Run early in the morning. When the attack was postponed, the men remained in position. Here they sweltered beneath a hot sun in the airless, unshaded ravine.

About 900 men remained after the previous day's battle. During July 1, Avery's men had marched shoulder to shoulder with Hays' Brigade in a victorious charge against the Federal rear guard at the almshouse line. According to Early, they had advanced 'in

HOKE'S (AVERY'S) BRIGADE
Colonel Isaac Erwin Avery/
Colonel Archibald Campbell Godwin

6th North Carolina State Troops
Major Samuel McDowell Tate
21st Regiment North Carolina Troops
Colonel William Whedbee Kirkland
57th Regiment North Carolina Troops
Colonel Archibald Campbell Godwin/
Successor's name not available

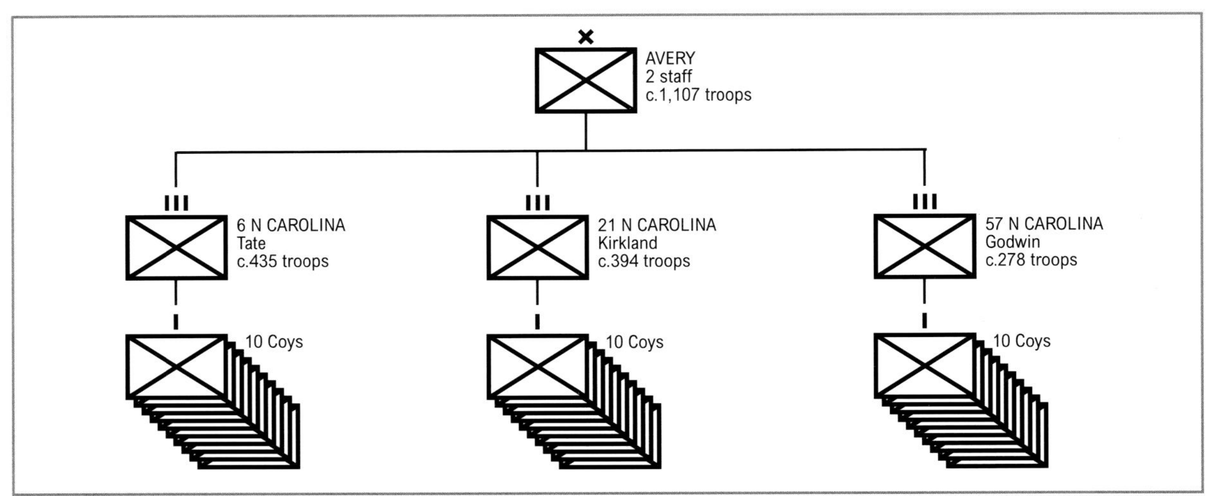

6th North Carolina State Troops

Co. A	Name not available
Co. B	Name not available
Co. C	Name not available
Co. D	Name not available
Co. E	Name not available
Co. F	Name not available
Co. G	Name not available
Co. H	Caswell Boys
Co. I	Cedar Fork Rifles
Co. K	Name not available

21st Regiment North Carolina Troops

Co. A	Davidson Guards
Co. C	Blue Ridge Riflemen
Co. D	Forsyth Rifles
Co. F	Mountain Boys
Co. G	Town Fork Invincibles
Co. H	Mountain Tigers
Co. I	Surry Marksmen
Co. K	Forsyth Southrons
Co. L	Rockingham Invincibles
Co. M	Guilford Dixie Boys

fine style, encountering and driving [the enemy] back into the town in great confusion.' The brigade had lost 22 killed and 123 wounded.

Federal sharpshooters pinned the brigade to the ravine. Colonel Avery and his aides, like the rest of the brigade, spent most of the time sitting or lying down. An aide recalls, 'the enemy sharpshooters kept us uneasy all the time' as their balls hissed overhead. At one point Avery laughingly commented that they had best move except there was no place better to go.

As it awaited the signal to charge, the brigade had the 6th North Carolina on its right, the 21st North Carolina in the centre, and the 57th North Carolina on the left near the Culp farm springhouse. A soldier recalls seeing officers appearing to ride rapidly from regiment to regiment. It was about 1930 hrs. Then Colonel Avery ordered, 'Forward, Guide Right' and the men climbed out of the ravine to begin their charge.

57th Regiment North Carolina Troops

Cos. A through K. All Company names not available

Smith's Brigade

During July 1, General Early retained Smith's Brigade in reserve to secure the division's left flank. When he twice ordered Smith to join the pursuit of the defeated Union XI Corps, Smith refused. He claimed that a large enemy force was threatening the flank and marched his men two miles along the York Pike to a position east of Gettysburg. The threat failed to materialise. An officer claimed that the 'enemy line' that Smith perceived was, in fact, a fence line!

The significance of Smith's erroneous claim was that

SMITH'S BRIGADE
Brigadier-General William Smith

31st Virginia Infantry Regiment
Colonel John Stringer Hoffman
49th Virginia Infantry Regiment
Lieutenant-Colonel Jonathan Catlett Gibson
52nd Virginia Infantry Regiment
Lieutenant-Colonel James H. Skinner

Brigadier-General William 'Extra Billy' Smith, 66, a former governor of Virginia, earned his nickname due to financial improprieties early in his career. Courageous and popular, he held West-Pointers in particular contempt. (USAMHI,Carlisle)

it caused Ewell to delay an assault against Cemetery Hill. To ensure his flank's safety, Ewell ordered Gordon's Brigade to march to support Smith. Thus, at a critical time on the evening of July 1, with the Confederate flood at full tide, half of Early's Division was involved in opposing a phantom menace.

Smith's Brigade remained in position about 2 1/2 miles east of Gettysburg on July 2. When a report came that Union cavalry was approaching, the brigade deployed to engage. Instead of contacting the enemy, the brigade encountered General Stuart.

Stuart ordered one Virginia regiment to remain in position to support part of his cavalry during the evening of July 2.

31st Virginia Infantry Regiment

Co. A	Marion Guard
Co. B	Captain Robert H. Bradshaw's Co.
Co. C	Captain Uriel M. Turner's Co.
Co. D	Gilmer Rifles
Co. E	The Highlanders
Co. F	Captain Jacob Currence's Co.
Co. G	Captain James C. Arbogast's Co.
Co. H	Captain Albert G. Reger's Co.
Co. I	Captain Alfred H. Jackson's Co.
Co. K	Captain Henry Sturn's Co.

49th Virginia Infantry Regiment

Co. A	Ewell Guards
Co. B	Quantico Guards
Co. C	Fauquier Guards
Co. D	Warren Blues
Co. E	Flint Hill Rifles
Co. F	Captain William H. Crowder's Co.
Co. H	New Market Volunteers
Co. I	Amherst Rough and Readys
Co. K	Sperryville Sharp Shooters

52nd Virginia Infantry Regiment

Co. A	Augusta Fencibles
Co. B	Captain William Long's Co.
Co. C	Letcher Guard
Co. D	Captain Joseph F. Hottel's Co.
Co. E	Captain Thomas H. Watkin's Co.
Co. F	Captain Joseph E. Cline's Co.
Co. G	Captain Samuel McCune's Co.
Co. H	Staunton Pioneers
Co. I	Men of West Augusta
Co. K	Captain Benjamin J. Walton's Co.

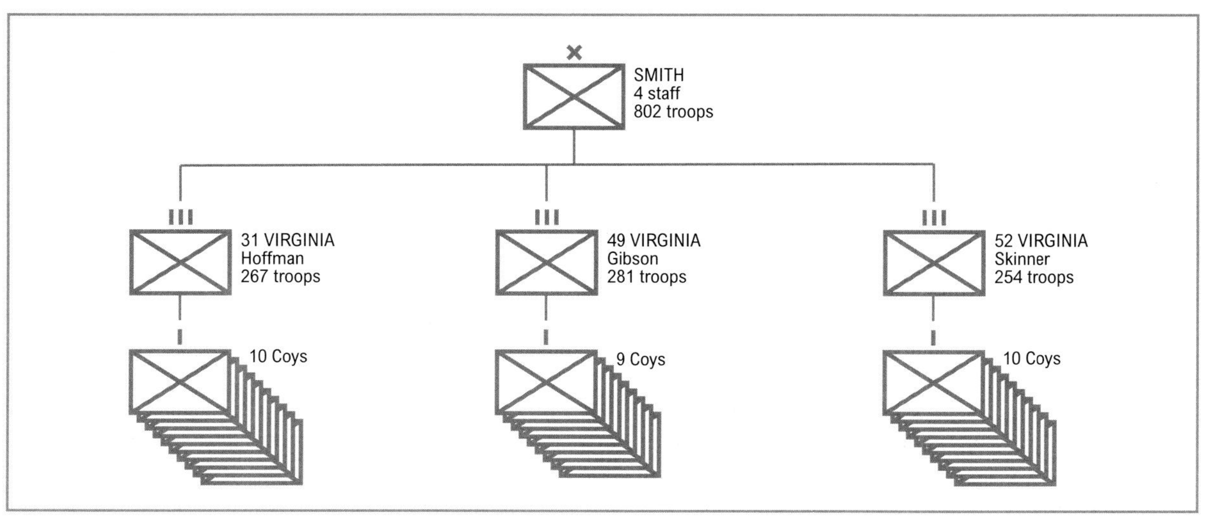

Gordon's Brigade

Gordon's Brigade suffered the brunt of the division's losses on July 1. The 13th Georgia lost 103 men; the 26th, 11; the 31st, 43; the 38th, 91; the 60th, 37 and the 61st, 93. The entire brigade lost 70 killed, 269 wounded, and 39 missing for a total of 586, a loss rate of more than one in four.

Brigadier-General John Brown Gordon, was a charismatic commander. On July 2, he was to support Hays' and Avery's Brigades during their attack on Cemetery Hill. When this faltered, Gordon's Brigade was recalled before it could engage. (MARS)

GORDON'S BRIGADE
Brigadier-General John Brown Gordon

13th Regiment Georgia Volunteer Infantry
Colonel James Milton Smith
26th Regiment Georgia Volunteer Infantry
Colonel Edmund Nathan Atkinson
31st Regiment Georgia Volunteer Infantry
Colonel Clement Anselm Evans
38th Regiment Georgia Volunteer Infantry
Captain William L. McLeod
60th Regiment Georgia Volunteer Infantry
Captain Waters Burras Jones
61st Regiment Georgia Volunteer Infantry
Colonel John Hill Lamar

Then and thereafter, Gordon believed that the Army of Northern Virginia stood on the verge of victory. All that was required was one more push against the high ground south of Gettysburg. Instead, Brigadier-General William Smith reported the presence of a hostile force approaching the army's flank from the east. Early and Ewell doubted the veracity of Smith's report. However, Early decided to reinforce Smith with Gordon's Brigade. Gordon protested vehemently but to no avail. Instead of participating in a possibly war- clinching charge against Cemetery Hill, his men turned their backs on the battle and marched off to support Smith against a force that never materialised. No one knew that Gordon's men were to participate no more in the battle.

On July 2, when a report came that Union cavalry was advancing against Smith's Brigade, Gordon's men

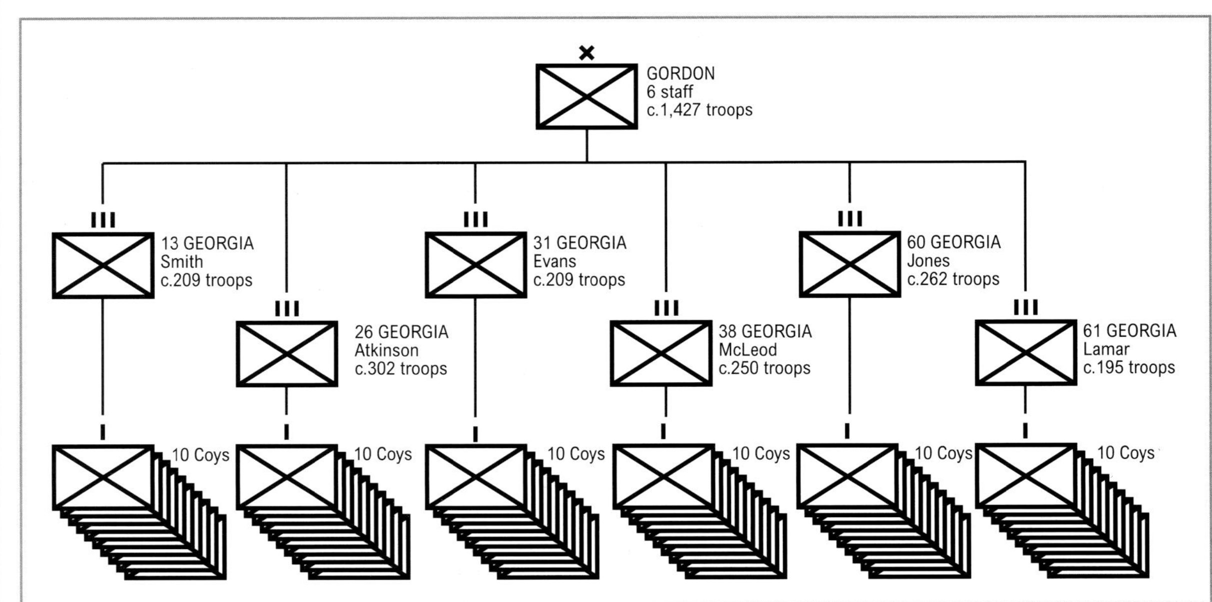

13th Regiment Georgia Volunteer Infantry	
Co. A	Confederate Guards
Co. B	Meriwether Volunteers
Co. C	Ringgold Rangers
Co. D	Upson Volunteers
Co. E	Randolph Volunteers
Co. F	Fayette Rangers
Co. G	Early Guards
Co. H	Panola Rifles
Co. I	Stark Volunteers
Co. K	Evans Guards

marched out along the York Pike to support Smith. In the event, Smith did not require support.

In the early afternoon, when Early learned that a demonstration in favour of Longstreet would begin at about 1600 hrs, he recalled Gordon so he could participate in the attack against Cemetery Hill. Gordon arrived and Early placed him along the railroad track east of Gettysburg about one-quarter mile behind the two brigades positioned in the ravine along Winebrenner's Run.

26th Regiment Georgia Volunteer Infantry	
Co. A	Brunswick Riflemen
Co. B	McIntosh County Guards
Co. C	Piscola Volunteers
Co. D	Seaboard Guards
Co. E	Wiregrass Minute Men
Co. F	Ware Guards
Co. G	Okefenokee Rifles
Co. H	Bartow Light Infantry
Co. I	Faulk Invincibles
Co. K	Forest Rangers

Early related in his official report that when Hays and Avery advanced, 'Gordon's brigade was ordered forward to support them, and did advance to the position from which they had moved, but was halted, here because it was ascertained that no advance was made on the right [by Rodes' Division] and it was evident that the crest of the hill could not be held by my brigades supported by this one without any assistance, and that the attempt would be attended with a useless sacrifice of life.' Therefore, Early recalled Gordon's Brigade before it engaged.

31st Regiment Georgia Volunteer Infantry	
Co. A	Georgia Light Infantry
Co. B	Muscogee Confederates
Co. C	Mitchell Guards
Co. D	Monroe Crowders
Co. E	Bartow Guards
Co. F	Pulaski Blues
Co. G	Name not available
Co. H	Mountain Tigers
Co. I	Arnet Rifles
Co. K	Bartow Avengers

38th Regiment Georgia Volunteer Infantry	
Co. A	Murphey Guards
Co. B	Milton Guards
Co. C	Ben Hill Guards
Co. D	McCullough Rifles
Co. E	Tom Cobb Infantry
Co. F	Thornton Volunteers
Co. G	Batley Guards
Co. H	Goshen Blues
Co. I	Irwin Invincibles
Co. K	Bartow Avengers

If Gordon's six regiments had advanced promptly to support the attack on Cemetery Hill, their presence may well have tipped the balance. Some of the survivors of Avery's Brigade had no doubt. Gordon himself sensed that his brigade had not done all it should on July 2. In his official report, after describing the glorious action of July 1, he wrote: 'The movements during the succeeding days of the battle (July 2 and 3), I do not consider of sufficient importance to mention.'

60th Regiment Georgia Volunteer Infantry	
Co. A	Anthony Grays
Co. B	Fannin Guards
Co. C	Walker Independents
Co. D	Whitfield Volunteers
Co. E	Bartow Avengers
Co. F	Gilmer Volunteers
Co. G	Dooly Guards
Co. H	Name not available
Co. I	Name not available
Co. K	Name not available

61st Regiment Georgia Volunteer Infantry	
Co. A	Irwin Cowboys
Co. B	Tattnall Rangers
Co. C	Wiregrass Rifles
Co. D	DeKalb Guards
Co. E	Montgomery Sharpshooters
Co. F	Stark Guards
Co. G	Wilkes Guards
Co. H	Tattnall County Volunteers
Co. I	Thompson Guards
Co. K	Name not available

Divisional Artillery – Jones' Battalion of Artillery

July 1 had been an active day for the divisional artillery battalion commanded by Lieutenant-Colonel Hilary Jones. The battalion was composed of four, four-gun batteries, equally divided between rifled and smooth bore Napoleon pieces. It arrived north of Gettysburg to find Rodes' Division heavily engaged. General Early ordered Jones to deploy immediately. Jones reported that he 'placed twelve guns in position, and opened fire with considerable effect on the enemy's artillery, and upon the flank of a column of troops'.

The battalion lost one killed and one wounded. However, three guns were temporarily disabled by having shots wedged in the bores. One Napoleon was permanently disabled after a yankee solid shot struck and bent its muzzle. The gunners successfully fixed the three guns while a captured Napoleon replaced the disabled gun.

On July 2, the Chief of Artillery for II Corps, Colonel J. Thompson Brown, had five artillery battalions at his disposal. When he examined the ground he could find positions on which to deploy only two of them. Jones' was not one of the battalions that Brown selected. Instead, the battalion held its position north of Gettysburg. Its orders were to defend against a 'reported flank movement of the enemy on our left.'

At 1500 hrs, Brigadier-General Smith, on detached duty to guard the division's rear, requested assistance. Captain William Tanner took his Courtney Artillery to help Smith but did not see action.

The rest of the battalion continued on guard duty until Brown received a request from General James Stuart to send artillery to assist General Hampton's cavalry at Hunterstown. Hunterstown was a small hamlet five miles northeast of Gettysburg. Stuart's column had passed through around noon. Thereafter, Union troopers had driven a detachment of Hampton's men from the hamlet. Fearful that this was a prelude to a cavalry thrust against Lee's left flank, Hampton had asked for help.

BATTALION EQUIPMENT
19 Caissons
221 Horses
2 Forges

Jones' Battalion had eight 12-pounder Napoleon smoothbores under command. (MARS)

Just before sunset, Captain Charles Green moved the Louisiana Guard Artillery's section of 10-pounder Parrott rifles some three miles to a position outside Hunterstown where he reported to Hampton. The section arrived at dusk and immediately engaged a Union horse artillery battery. The duel lasted until dark at which point the section retired about one mile. In his official report, Hampton wrote that the section 'did good service.'

Jones' Battalion of Artillery
Lieutenant-Colonel Hilary Pollard Jones
9 Staff and Field Officers

Charlottesville Artillery (Virginia)
Captain James McDowell Carrington
4 x 12-pounder Napoleon guns
(71 troops present for duty equipped)
Courtney Artillery (Virginia)
Captain William A. Tanner
4 x 3-inch rifled guns
(90 troops present for duty equipped)
Louisiana Guard Battery
Captain Charles A. Green
2 x 3-inch rifled guns
2 x 10-pounder Parrott rifled guns
(60 troops present for duty equipped)
Staunton Artillery (Virginia)
Captain Asher Waterman Garber
4 x 12-pounder Napoleon guns
(60 troops present for duty equipped)

II Corps – Johnson's Division

Major-General Edward Johnson's Division approached Gettysburg on the Chambersburg Pike on July 1. After ascending the Cashtown Gap, the men could hear the sounds of battle. They increased their pace and arrived on Seminary Ridge about sundown.

Because Ewell believed that Culp's Hill was unoccupied, he ordered Johnson to seize the hill if possible. The division moved east and then south, marching almost all of the way to the Hanover Road. Here it deployed in a single line of brigades, facing south and about one mile from Culp's Hill. Scouts reported the hill occupied so Johnson ordered his men to sleep in place.

Major-General Edward Johnson was new to the Army of Northern Virginia. He failed to occupy Culp's Hill on July 1, but his division was tasked with the assault on the Federal positions there on the evening of July 2. (MARS)

JOHNSON'S DIVISION
Major-General Edward Johnson

Steuart's Brigade - 2,116 troops
Stonewall (Walker's) Brigade - 1,319 troops
Nicholls' (Williams') Brigade - 1,101 troops
Jones' Brigade - 1,560 troops
Latimer's Artillery Battalion - 347 troops

The revised plan for July 2 required Johnson's Division to begin its diversion in favour of Longstreet after I Corps attacked the Federal left. During the day, Walker's Brigade became involved in a skirmish with Union cavalry on Brinkerhoff's Ridge. The three remaining brigades deployed in the order: Jones on the right, Nicholls in the middle and Steuart on the left.

They knew that the enemy was digging in and it worried them. A major recalled, 'Greatly did officers and men marvel as the morning, noon and afternoon passed in inaction on our part, not on the enemy's.'

At about 1700 hrs, Johnson's artillery commenced its bombardment of Culp's Hill and Jones' Brigade moved forward to support the artillery on Benner's Hill.

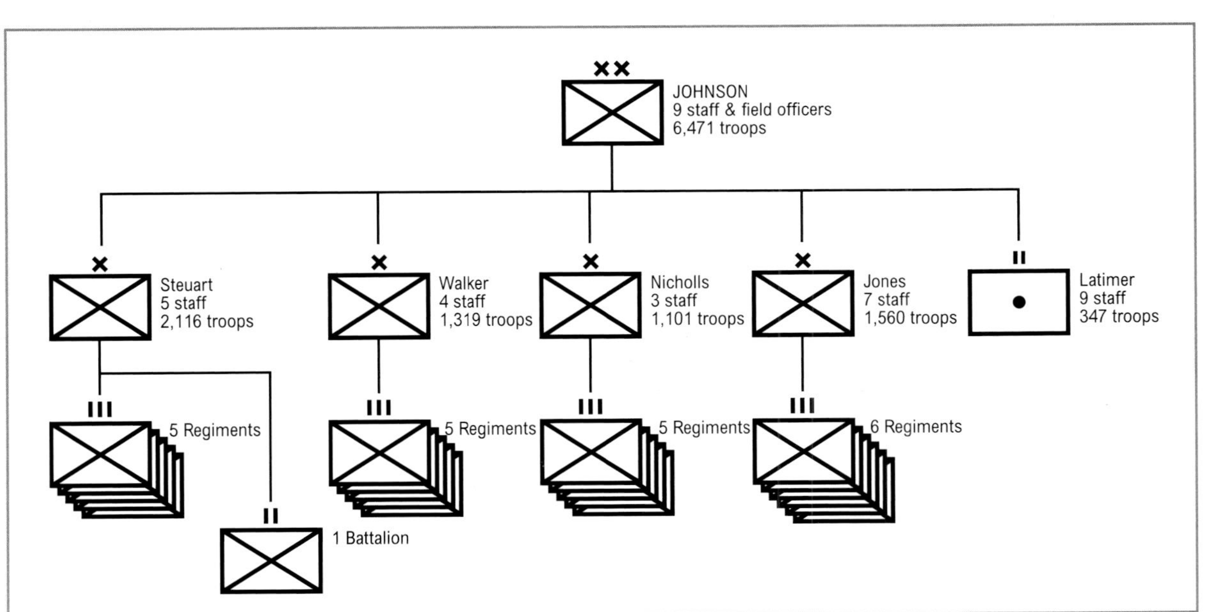

Steuart's Brigade

Brigadier-General George Steuart and his men arose early on July 2 to attack Culp's Hill. After several anxious hours, they learned that the attack was postponed until the afternoon.

The brigade remained under shelter in the woods on Wolf's Hill until an artillery task force commanded by Major Latimer opened fire. Then it formed in battle array and awaited the signal to advance. The 23rd Virginia entered the battle understrength. Four companies were detached on skirmish duty and two more were acting as 'brigade guard', presumably in a provost detail.

In order to take its place on the left of the divisional line, the brigade was forced to wheel to the southwest. The 3rd North Carolina's effort to maintain contact with the centre brigade (Nicholls) caused the other regiments to diverge from the line. Moreover, as they

Brigadier-General George Hume Steuart served as a cavalryman on the frontier. Lee expected the 35-year-old Marylander, a stern disciplinarian, to take control of a trouble-ridden brigade that was new to him. (USAMHI, Carlisle)

STEUART'S BRIGADE
Brigadier-General George Hume Steuart

1st Battalion Maryland Infantry
Lieutenant-Colonel James R. Herbert/
Major William Worthington Goldsborough/
Captain John W. Torsch
Captain James Parran Crane
1st North Carolina State Troops
Lieutenant-Colonel Hamilton Allen Brown
3rd North Carolina State Troops
Major William Murdoch Parsley
10th Virginia Infantry Regiment
Colonel Edward Tiffin Harrison Warren
23rd Virginia Infantry Regiment
Lieutenant-Colonel Simeon Taylor Walton
37th Virginia Infantry Regiment
Major Henry Clinton Wood

1st Battalion Maryland Infantry

Cos. C, D, E & I. All Company names not available.

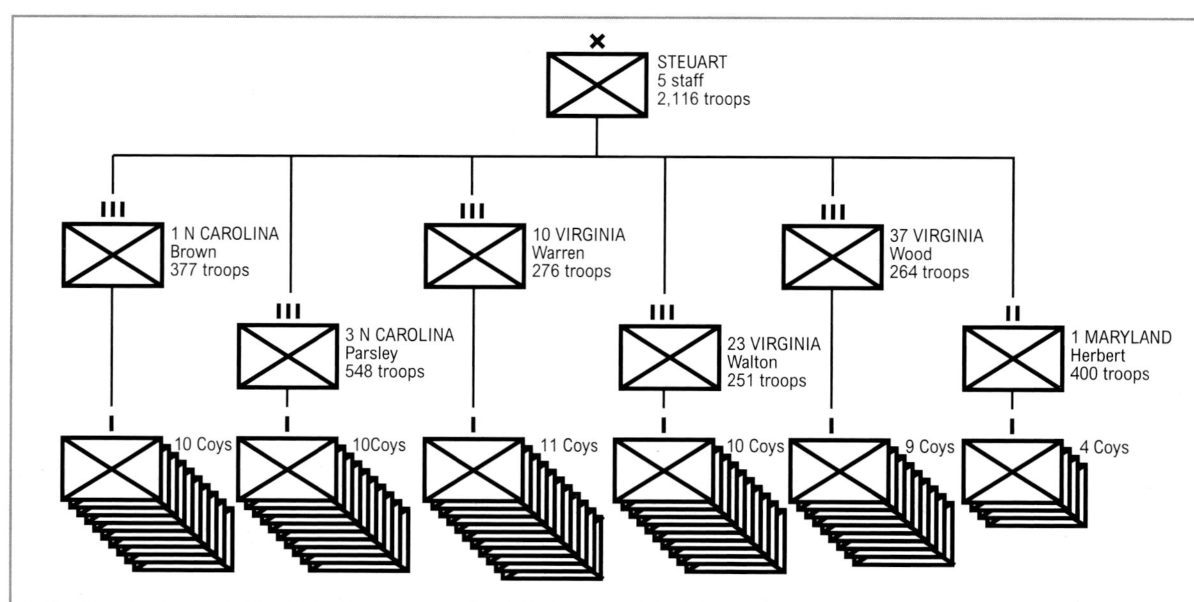

1st North Carolina State Troops

Co. A	Albemarle Guards
Co. B	Wilkes Volunteers
Co. C	Lillington Rifle Guards
Co. D	Name not available
Co. E	Name not available
Co. F	Hertford Greys
Co. G	Washington Volunteers
Co. H	Name not available
Co. I	Wake Light Infantry
Co. K	Name not available

approached Rock Creek the brigade had to traverse difficult ground. The trees and rocks on Wolf's Hill compelled officers to leave their horses behind and proceed on foot. Because of the effort to maintain alignment and due to the rough ground, the brigade's left did not cross the creek until its right had already waded it and begun its assault.

By the time the soldiers began their uphill climb, it was dark beneath the forest canopy that covered the slope of Culp's Hill. The Confederates on the brigade's right groped blindly ahead until greeted by a sheet of musketry fire.

3rd North Carolina State Troops

Co. A	Greene County Riflemen
Co. B	Name not available
Co. C	Name not available
Co. D	Name not available
Co. E	Onslow Greys
Co. F	Name not available
Co. G	Name not available
Co. H	Bladen Volunteers
Co. I	Jeff Davis' Rifles
Co. K	Holly Shelter Volunteers

10th Virginia Infantry Regiment

Co. A	Strasburg Guards
Co. B	Rockingham Rifles
Co. C	Captain Robert. C. Mauck's Co.
Co. D	Bridgewater Grays
Co. E	Peaked Mountain Grays
Co. F	Muhlenburg Rifles
Co. G	Valley Guards
Co. H	Chrisman's Infantry
Co. I	Riverton Invincibles
Co. K	Page Volunteers
Co. L	Jeff Davis Guard

23rd Virginia Infantry Regiment

Co. A	Louisa Rifles
Co. B	Jetersville Grays
Co. C	Amelia Rifles
Co. D	Louisa Grays
Co. E	Brooklyn Grays
Co. F	Goochland Grays
Co. G	Frederick's Hall Grays
Co. H	Richmond Sharpshooters
Co. I	Central Guards
Co. K	Keysville Guard

37th Virginia Infantry Regiment

Co. A	Goodson Rifle Guards
Co. B	Virginia Mountain Boys
Co. C	Captain John F. McElhenny's Co.
Co. D	Davis Rifle Guards
Co. E	Walnut Hill Co.
Co. F	Glade Spring Rifles
Co. G/I	Captain Cornelius A. Bussey's Co.
Co. H	King's Mountain Rifles
Co. K	Washington Independents

Stonewall (Walker's) Brigade

Along Hanover road at Brinkerhoff's Ridge, 2 1/2 miles east of Gettysburg, Brigadier-General James Walker's 'Stonewall Brigade' guarded the army's left flank.

It occupied a position along the eastern slope of the ridge where it skirmished with a variety of Federal forces who were moving to join the Union army. This should have been a job for J.E.B Stuart's troopers. Even a man in the ranks understood this, commenting that screening flanks was properly the duty of the 'absent, truant, cavalry'.

The first contact came at daybreak when skirmish-

STONEWALL (WALKER'S) BRIGADE
Brigadier-General James Alexander Walker

2nd Virginia Infantry Regiment
Colonel John Quincy Adams Nadenbousch
4th Virginia Infantry Regiment
Major William Terry
5th Virginia Infantry Regiment
Colonel John Henry Stover Funk
27th Virginia Infantry Regiment
Lieutenant-Colonel Daniel McKeloran Shriver
33rd Virginia Infantry Regiment
Captain Jacob Burner Golladay

Brigadier-General James Alexander Walker assumed command of the Stonewall Brigade after Chancellorsville. Ironically, as a VMI senior he had challenged Stonewall Jackson to a duel and been expelled. (MARS)

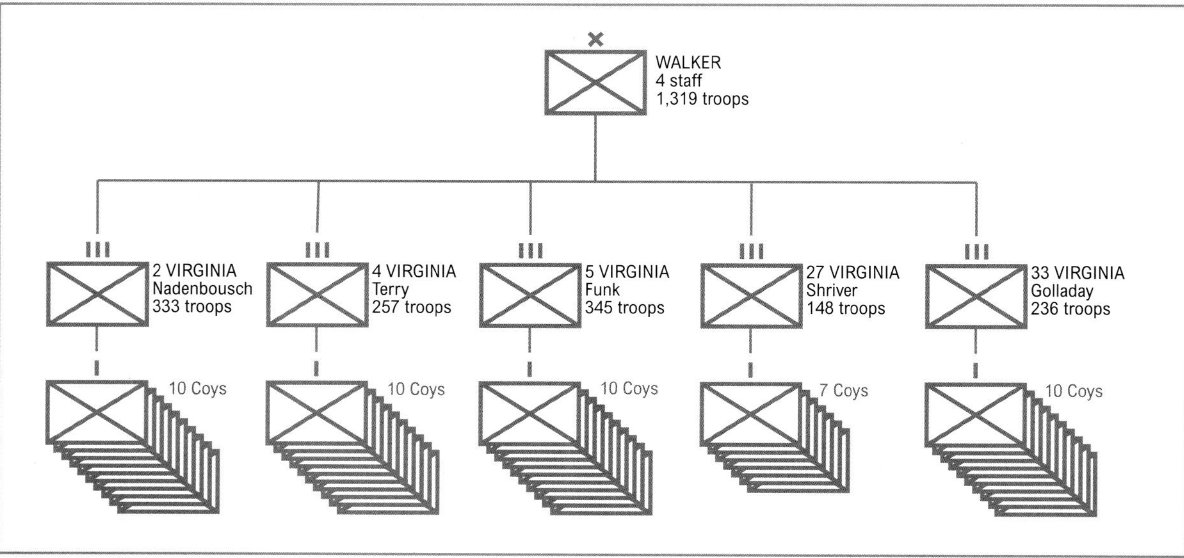

ers from a Federal brigade that had spent the night camped nearby encountered rebel skirmishers on the north slope of Wolf's Hill. The Confederates held a position stretching from a barn and stone house into the woods. To their front was another group of buildings that both sides sought to capture.

Shortly thereafter, Federal V Corps moved into the area by way of the Hanover Road. The shuffling of Union units continued throughout the morning. Meanwhile, the Stonewall Brigade skirmishers fought with whichever enemy units appeared to its front. A Virginia sergeant recalls how the rebel skirmishers would lay flat on the ground, load their rifles while lying on their backs, and then roll over onto their stomachs

2nd Virginia Infantry Regiment

Co. A	Jefferson Guards
Co. B	Hamtramck Guards
Co. C	Nelson Guards
Co. D	Berkeley Border Guards
Co. E	Hedgesville Blues
Co. F	Winchester Rifles
Co. G	Botts' Grays
Co. H	Letcher Riflemen
Co. I	Clarke Riflemen
Co. K	Floyd Guards

4th Virginia Infantry Regiment

Co. A	Wythe Grays
Co. B	Fort Lewis Volunteers
Co. C	Pulaski Guards
Co. D	Smyth Blues
Co. E	Montgomery Highlanders
Co. F	Grayson Daredevils
Co. G	Montgomery Fencibles
Co. H	Rockbridge Grays
Co. I	Liberty Hall Volunteers
Co. L	Captain Robert G. Newlee's Co.

5th Virginia Infantry Regiment

Co. A	Marion Rifles
Co. C	Mountain Guard
Co. D	Southern Guard
Co. E	Augusta Grays
Co. F	West View Infantry
Co. G	Staunton Rifles
Co. H	Augusta Rifles
Co. I	Ready Rifles of Augusta County
Co. K	Continental Morgan Guards
Co. L	West Augusta Guard

to aim and fire. The most significant encounter occurred in the afternoon when the 2nd Virginia fought the dismounted cavalry of Gregg's Division. In an escalating encounter that began at around 1600 hrs, Walker ordered the Virginians to 'clear the field' of opposing skirmishers. The 2nd charged a contested stone wall. Its effort apparently lacked conviction since the regiment suffered only three men wounded. By dusk the fighting ended.

27th Virginia Infantry Regiment

Co. B	Virginia Hibernians
Co. C	Alleghany Rifles
Co. D	Monroe Guard
Co. E	Greenbrier (Lewisburg) Rifles
Co. F	Greenbrier Sharp Shooters
Co. G	Shriver Greys
Co. H	Rockbridge Rifles

33rd Virginia Infantry Regiment

Co. A	Potomac Guards
Co. B	Toms Brook Guard
Co. C	Tenth Legion Minute Men
Co. D	Mountain Rangers
Co. E	Emerald Guard
Co. F	Independent Greys
Co. G	Mount Jackson Rifles
Co. H	Page Grays
Co. I	Rockingham Confederates
Co. K	Shenandoah Sharpshooters

Nicholls' (Williams') Brigade

At the battle of Chancellorsville on May 2, 1863, Brigadier-General Francis Nicholls suffered a serious shell wound resulting in the loss of his foot. The brigade's senior colonel, Jesse Williams, assumed command.

Williams' rise to command came from attrition rather than his own shining qualities. At Malvern Hill the then Captain Williams was the senior surviving officer in his 2nd Louisiana Regiment. He received promotion to regimental command. At Second Manassas the brigade achieved renown while defending the railroad cut. Low on ammunition, the Louisiana soldiers hurled rocks at the charging yankees. At Sharpsburg Williams received a serious chest wound and was captured. He was exchanged in time for the Chancell-orsville Campaign and thus assumed brigade command in time for the fight on May 3.

The brigade performed poorly under Williams' leadership. At a critical time, Williams was unable to get his men to charge. Worse, they almost lost their own

NICHOLLS' (WILLIAMS') BRIGADE
Colonel Jesse Milton Williams

1st Louisiana Infantry Regiment
Lieutenant-Colonel Michael Nolan
2nd Louisiana Infantry Regiment
Lieutenant-Colonel Ross E. Burke
10th Louisiana Infantry Regiment
Major Thomas N. Powell
14th Louisiana Infantry Regiment
Lieutenant-Colonel David Zable
15th Louisiana Infantry Regiment
Major Andrew Brady

1st Louisiana Infantry Regiment

Co. A	Caddo Rifles
Co. B	Red River Rebels
Co. C	Slocumb Rifles
Co. D	Emmet Guards
Co. E	Montgomery Guards
Co. F	Orleans Light Guards, Co. D
Co. G	Orleans Light Guards, Co. B
Co. I	Orleans Light Guards, Co. A
Co. K	Orleans Light Guards, Co. C

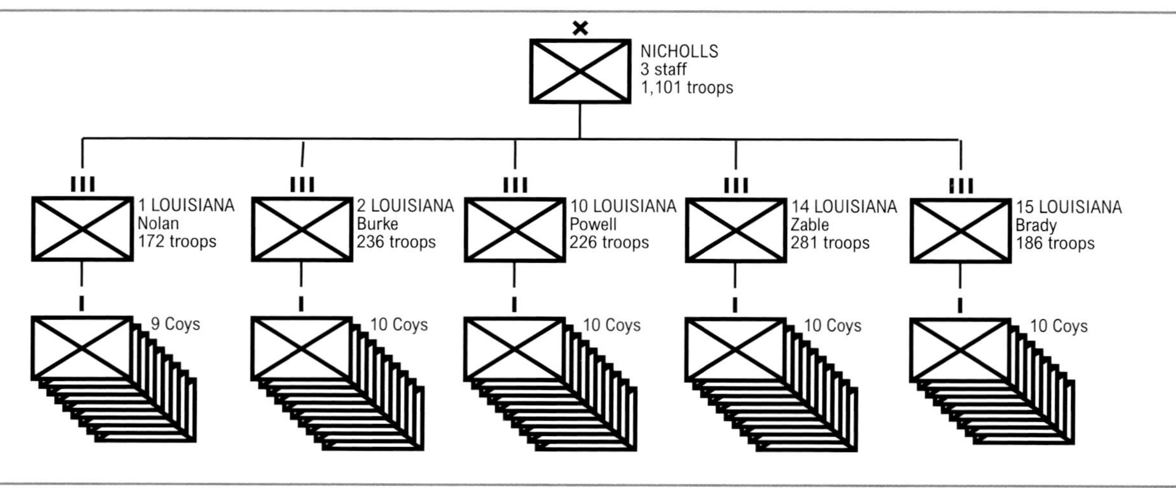

2nd Louisiana Infantry Regiment

Co. A	Lecompte Guards
Co. B	Moore Guards
Co. C	Pelican Greys
Co. D	Pelican Rifles
Co. E	Vernon Guards
Co. F	Claiborne Guards
Co. G	Floyd Guards
Co. H	Atchafalaya Guards
Co. I	Greenwood Guards
Co. K	Vienna Rifles

14th Louisiana Infantry Regiment

Co. A	Armstrong Guards
Co. B	Jefferson Cadets
Co. C	Askew Guards
Co. D	McClure Guards
Co. E	Nixon Rifles
Co. F	Concordia Rifles
Co. G	Avengo Rifles
Co. H	Quitman Rangers
Co. I	Tiger Bayou Rifles
Co. K	Lafayette Rifle Cadets

Battle flag of Lieutenant-Colonel Ross Burke's 2nd Louisiana Infantry Regiment.

position until saved by a rebel counter-attack.

General Lee cast about for an alternative brigade commander but could not locate one. Constant combat had seriously depleted the well of capable brigade commanders. Consequently, Williams continued to lead the brigade during the invasion of Pennsylvania.

Like the other leaders in Johnson's Division, Williams had his men up early on July 2 in order to be ready to assault Culp's Hill. When the stand-down order came the brigade relaxed under the trees of Wolf's Hill. The brigade formed the centre unit in Johnson's assault against Culp's Hill.

10th Louisiana Infantry Regiment

Co. A	Shepherd Guards
Co. B	Derbigny Guards
Co. C	Hewitt Guards
Co. D	Hawkins Guards
Co. E	Louisiana Swamp Rifles
Co. F	Louisiana Rebels
Co. G	Orleans Rangers
Co. H	Orleans Blues
Co. I	Tirailleurs D'Orleans
Co. K	Confederate States Rangers

15th Louisiana Infantry Regiment

Co. A	Askew Guards, Co. B
Co. B	Empire Rangers
Co. C	Gross Tete Creoles
Co. D	St. Ceran Rifles
Co. E	Grivot Rifles
Co. F	Saint James Rifles
Co. G	Davenport Rebels
Co. H	Bogart Guards
Co. I	Catahoula Guerillas
Co. K	Crescent City Blues, Co. B

Jones' Brigade

When Latimer's guns opened fire against Culp's Hill, Johnson ordered Brigadier-General John Marshall Jones to advance to support the artillery. It was the first combat manoeuvre of an inexperienced officer, new to both this Virginia Brigade and to brigade command.

The Virginia Brigade had performed poorly at Chancellorsville. Its commanding officer had excused himself from leadership at a time when the brigade was involved in heavy fighting. It subsequently refused to charge, compelling the supporting brigade literally to step over its prone ranks to execute the attack. The six regiments that comprised Jones' Brigade required good leadership and discipline after their disgraceful behaviour at Chancellorsville.

General Lee cast about for a replacement and selected Jones, an officer who previously had been praised as 'gallant and efficient' while performing his

JONES' BRIGADE
Brigadier-General John Marshall Jones/
Lieutenant-Colonel Robert H. Dungan

21st Virginia Infantry Regiment
Captain William Perkins Moseley
25th Virginia Infantry Regiment
Colonel John Carlton Higginbotham/
Lieutenant-Colonel John Armstead Robinson
42nd Virginia Infantry Regiment
Lieutenant-Colonel Robert Woodson Withers/
Captain S.H. Saunders
44th Virginia Infantry Regiment
Colonel Norvell Cobb/
Captain T.A. Buckner
48th Virginia Infantry Regiment
Lieutenant-Colonel Robert H. Dungan/
Major Oscar White
50th Virginia Infantry Regiment
Lieutenant-Colonel Logan Henry Neal Salyer

A West Point graduate, Brigadier-General John Marshall Jones had combined poor study habits with heavy drinking, earning the nickname 'Rum' Jones. He served in the Mexican War and in various staff positions until after the Battle of Chancellorsville. (MARS)

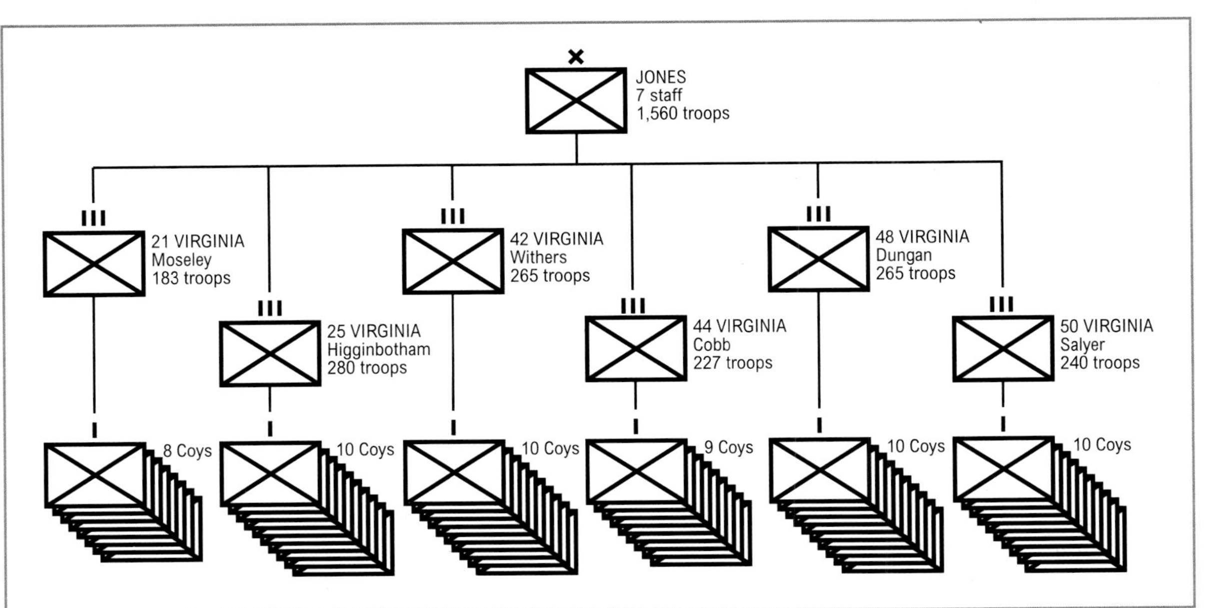

21st Virginia Infantry Regiment	
Co. A	Red House Volunteers
Co. C	Oliver Grays
Co. D	Cumberland Greys
Co. E	Buckingham Leaches
Co. G	Brunswick Grays
Co. H	Chalk Level Grays
Co. I	Turkey Cock Grays
Co. K	Meherrin Greys

44th Virginia Infantry Regiment	
Co. B	Byrd Rifles
Co. C	Travis Rifles
Co. D	Ambler Grays
Co. E	Richmond Zouaves
Co. F	Fluvanna Hornets
Co. G	Randolph Guard
Co. H	Amelia Minute Men
Co. I	Mossingford Rifles
Co. K	Fluvanna Guards

staff duties. However, when recommending Jones, Lee wrote to President Davis, 'Should he fail in his duty, he will instantly resign.' There is little doubt that Lee was referring to 'Rum' Jones' great proclivity for the bottle.

On July 1 the brigade led Johnson's column as it marched along the Chambersburg Pike to Gettysburg.

25th Virginia Infantry Regiment	
Co. A	Letcher Guard
Co. B	Upshur Grays
Co. C	Braxton Blues
Co. D	Augusta Lee Rifles
Co. E	Franklin Guards
Co. F	Highland Rangers
Co. G	Captain William H. Mollohan's Co.
Co. H	Rockbridge Guards
Co. I	Pocahontas Rescues
Co. K	Pendleton Minutemen

It moved to a position facing Culp's Hill but did not see action. When the assault was postponed, four companies of the 25th Virginia went forward as skirmishers and the rest of the brigade rested.

On July 2, after Johnson ordered the brigade to support Latimer's gunners, the presence of yankee marksmen and their accurate fire at the Confederate artillerymen prompted Jones to commit the rest of the 25th into the skirmish line. His remaining regiments occupied a position about 300 yards to the left and behind the artillery gun line. Johnson instructed Jones to advance when Nicholls' Brigade marched up to his left flank. Because of the terrain, the brigade had to advance directly at Culp's Hill. Also, because its objective was covered in thick trees, no one had much of an idea about the strength and disposition of the defenders. The brigade probably aligned on a rail fence that ran southwest and down the slope of Benner's Hill. The exact sequence of regiments is unknown. As the Virginians crossed a shallow portion of Rock Creek they received heavy skirmish fire. Jones halted his brigade to dress ranks and then charged up the slope.

48th Virginia Infantry Regiment	
Co. A	Stock Creek Greys
Co. B	Campbell Guards
Co. C	Osborne Ford Independents
Co. D	Smyth Rifle Greys
Co. E	Nickelsville Spartan Band
Co. F	Holston Foresters
Co. G	Lee County Guards
Co. H	Clinch Mountain Boomers
Co. I	Mountain Marksmen
Co. K	Russell Guards

42nd Virginia Infantry Regiment	
Co. A	Henry Volunteers
Co. B	Floyd Guards
Co. C	Buford Grays
Co. D	Campbell-Lee Guards
Co. E	Dixie Grays
Co. F	Leatherwood Fencibles
Co. G	Captain William W. Morris' Co.
Co. H	Patrick Henry Volunteers
Co. I	Campbell Guards
Co. K	Franklin Invincibles

50th Virginia Infantry Regiment	
Co. A	Lee Rifles
Co. B	Captain Alexander S. Vandeventer's Co.
Co. C	Captain Francis White Kelly's Co.
Co. D	Wilson Rifles
Co. E	Smyth Grays
Co. F	Pedlar Mills Guard
Co. G	Captain William S. Hannah's Co.
Co. H	Wise Yankee Catchers
Co. I	Captain Thomas Poage's Co.
Co. K	Patrick Boys

Divisional Artillery - Latimer's Battalion of Artillery

During the Gettysburg Campaign, Major Joseph W. Latimer commanded the battalion in the place of the wounded Lieutenant-Colonel Andrews. After a tiring march of over 20 miles, the battalion parked in a wheat field east of Gettysburg on the night of July 1.

At 0400 hrs on July 2, Latimer set off to find a position to deploy his guns. He selected Benner's Hill south of the Hanover Road as the best available position. With a gun line established on its bare crest, batteries could fire effectively on Cemetery Hill but only the left-hand battery could bombard Culp's Hill. Since Federal guns overlooked this exposed site, Latimer resolved to delay deployment until his guns were needed.

Unlike many battalions, Latimer's men did not have to crew short-range, smoothbore weapons in their struggle to gain fire superiority. (Author's Collection)

In an army full of meritorious artillerymen, the 19-year-old Latimer shone. Ewell called him the 'Young Napoleon'. Soldiers called him 'The Boy Major' and often cheered him when he rode by.

Reputedly, General Johnson ordered Major William Goldsborough, whom he presumed possessed local knowledge, to examine Benner's Hill and to assess its suitability as an artillery position. Goldsborough scouted the position, concluded that enemy guns dominated it and thus it should not be occupied, but before he could report to Johnson, Latimer received an order from the divisional general to advance and to 'open fire with all his pieces.'

The battalion advanced in splendid style. An eye-witness related, 'Sixteen guns, sixteen caissons, with their attending cavalcade of company and field officers, streaming over the field in bustle and busy speed and enveloped in clouds of dust.' A Maryland gunner recalls that Latimer rode to the front of the gun line, raised his sword, called the unit to attention, and ordered it to open fire.

BATTALION EQUIPMENT

15 Caissons
124 Horses
2 Forges
1 Battery Wagon

Latimer's Battalion of Artillery
Major Joseph W. Latimer/
Captain Charles I. Raine
9 Staff and Field Officers

1st Maryland Battery
Captain William F. Dement
4 x 12-pounder Napoleon guns
(90 troops present for duty equipped)

Alleghany Artillery (Virginia)
Captain John Cadwalider Carpenter
2 x 3-inch rifled guns
2 x 12-pounder Napoleon guns
(91 troops present for duty equipped)

4th Chesapeake Artillery (Maryland)
Captain William D. Brown/
Successor's name not available
4 x 10-pounder howitzers
(76 troops present for duty equipped)

Lynchburg 'Lee' Artillery (Virginia)
Captain Charles I. Raine/
Lieutenant William W. Hardwicke
1 x 3-inch rifled gun
1 x 10-pounder Parrott rifled gun
2 x 20-pounder Parrott rifled guns
(90 troops present for duty equipped)

II Corps – Rodes' Division

At about 1415 hrs on July 1, Rodes' Division had found itself on the flank of the Union army. Sensing opportunity, Major-General Robert Rodes made a covered approach march through the woods of Oak Hill to deliver a flank attack. The division deployed on a three-brigade front with artillery support from Carter's Battalion stationed on Oak Hill.

The advance began when O'Neal's Brigade moved south along Oak Ridge and fell into a deadly trap. Then Iverson's Brigade advanced and fared even worse, losing 60 per cent of its strength. Daniel's Brigade was able to redeem these sorry performances by launching two charges against the railroad cut, culminating in a tactical envelopment that swept the field. Daniel's Brigade lost 37 per cent of its strength on July 1. Later, Doles' Brigade had cooperated with Early's Division to drive the Federal troops from Blocher's Knoll. Ramseur's Brigade also participated

RODES' DIVISION
(deployed but not engaged at Gettysburg on July 2)
Major-General Robert Emmett Rodes

DANIEL'S BRIGADE
Brigadier-General Junius Daniel
32nd Regiment North Carolina Troops
Colonel Edmund Crew Brabble
43rd Regiment North Carolina Troops
Colonel Thomas S. Kenan
45th Regiment North Carolina Troops
Major John R. Winston
53rd Regiment North Carolina Troops
Colonel William Allison Owens
2nd North Carolina Battalion
Captain Van Brown

DOLES' BRIGADE
Brigadier-General George Pierce Doles
4th Regiment Georgia Volunteer Infantry
Major William Henry Willis
12th Regiment Georgia Volunteer Infantry
Colonel Edward Willis
21st Regiment Georgia Volunteer Infantry
Colonel John Thomas Mercer
44th Regiment Georgia Volunteer Infantry
Major William Hubbard Peebles

IVERSON'S BRIGADE
Brigadier-General Alfred Iverson, Jr.
5th North Carolina State Troops
Captain Benjamin Robinson
12th Regiment North Carolina Troops
Lieutenant-Colonel William Smith Davis
20th Regiment North Carolina Troops
Captain Louis T. Hicks
23rd Regiment North Carolina Troops
Captain William H. Johnston

RAMSEUR'S BRIGADE
Brigadier-General Stephen Dodson Ramseur
2nd North Carolina State Troops
Captain James Turner Scales
4th Regiment North Carolina Troops
Colonel Bryan Grimes
14th Regiment North Carolina Troops
Colonel Risden Tyler Bennett
30th Regiment North Carolina Troops
Major William Walter Sillers

RODES' (O'NEAL'S) BRIGADE
Colonel Edward Asbury O'Neal
3rd Alabama Infantry Regiment
Colonel Cullen Andrews Battle
5th Alabama Infantry Regiment
Colonel Josephus Marion Hall
6th Alabama Infantry Regiment
Captain Milledge L. Bowie
12th Alabama Infantry Regiment
Colonel Samuel Bonneau Pickins
26th Alabama Infantry Regiment
Lieutenant-Colonel John Chapman Goodgame

CARTER'S BATTALION OF ARTILLERY
Lieutenant-Colonel Thomas Henry Carter
Jefferson Davis Artillery (Alabama)
Captain William J. Reese
King William Artillery (Virginia)
Captain William Pleasants Page Carter
Morris Artillery (Virginia)
Lieutenant Samuel H. Pendleton
Orange Artillery (Virginia)
Captain Charles William Fry

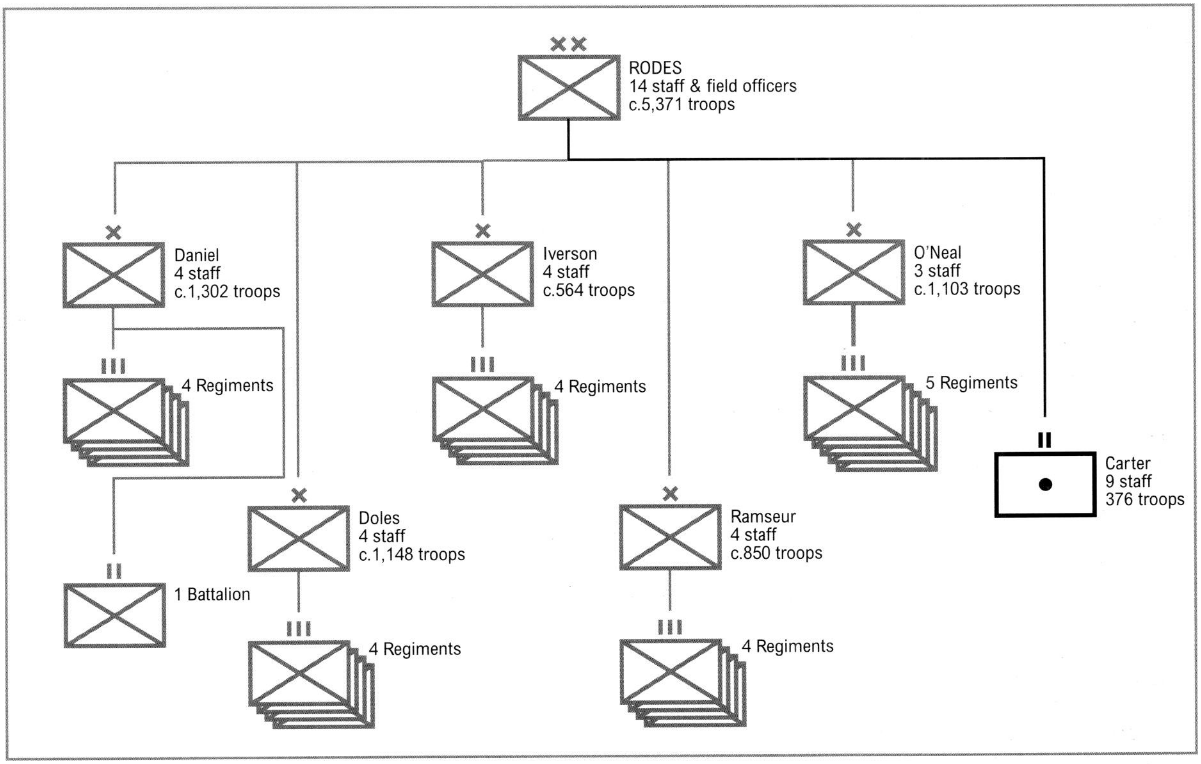

RODES
14 staff & field officers
c.5,371 troops

Daniel
4 staff
c.1,302 troops

4 Regiments

1 Battalion

Doles
4 staff
c.1,148 troops

4 Regiments

Iverson
4 staff
c.564 troops

4 Regiments

Ramseur
4 staff
c.850 troops

4 Regiments

O'Neal
3 staff
c.1,103 troops

5 Regiments

Carter
9 staff
376 troops

In his official report, Major-General Robert Emmett Rodes wrote: 'On July 2, nothing of importance transpired in my front.' Whether his inactivity was a blunder or merely a prudent decision remains one of the battle's great debates. (Carl Smith, Manassas)

in the triumphant final charge through the streets of Gettysburg. It too lost about 170 men.

In previous battles Rodes had displayed great talent as a regimental and brigade commander. July 1 at Gettysburg had witnessed a poorly coordinated attack caused by impetuous conduct, poor reconnaissance and inept performances by Iverson and O'Neal. Rodes was left with a division that had suffered significant losses with two brigades nearly shattered, one with moderate losses, and two with light casualties.

During the morning and afternoon of July 2, the division engaged in occasional skirmish combat and was subjected to 'Desultory firing of the opposing sharpshooters.' Confederate sharpshooters belonging to Doles' Brigade occupied houses in town whose back windows overlooked Cemetery Hill. They closed up the windows with mattresses and furniture and opened fire: 'a constant rattle of musketry by men stripped to the waist and blackened with powder' recalls an eyewitness.

In the afternoon Rodes received orders 'to co-operate with the attacking force as soon as any opportunity of doing so with good effect was offered.' Specifically, his division was to charge Cemetery Hill from the northwest while Early's Division assailed East Cemetery Hill.

Late in the afternoon Rodes detected movement on Cemetery Hill. He suspected that the yankees were shifting men to oppose Longstreet and judged that this movement presented an opportunity. After conferring with the adjacent divisional commanders, Rodes ordered his men to assemble. He would attack Cemetery Hill 'just at dark'.

In the event, he found that 'having to draw my troops out of town by the flank, change the direction of the line of battle, and then to traverse a distance of 1,200 to 1,400 yards' proved very time consuming. His line reached Long Lane, a position that provided a staging area for an attack against the northwest side of Cemetery Hill, by which time Early's attack had already failed. Rodes division did not engage that day.

II Corps' Reserve Artillery

The lack of suitable positions compelled II Corps' Chief of Artillery, Colonel J. Thompson Brown, to leave three artillery battalions in reserve. One of the battalions used at the front was the 1st Virginia Artillery Battalion of II Corps Artillery Reserve. The battalion was fresh, having arrived too late to engage on July 1.

To support the attack on Cemetery Hill on July 2, 12 pieces commanded by Captain Willis Dance occupied firing positions on Seminary Ridge. Captain David Watson's battery unlimbered north of the railroad cut. This was $1\frac{1}{2}$ miles from Cemetery Hill, a range too long to allow accurate fire. Captain Benjamin Smith's 3rd Richmond Howitzers deployed near the seminary while the Powhatan Artillery, commanded by Lieutenant John Cunningham, unlimbered south of the Fairfield Road. These two batteries were within a mile range of Cemetery Hill.

The battalion's 1st Rockbridge Artillery unlimbered its 20-pounder Parrott rifles on Benner's Hill north of the Hanover Road from where it could shell East Cemetery Hill. Before the action began, two 20-pounder Parrotts belonging to Raine's Lee Battery joined them to form a six-gun battery. At about 1600 hrs, the battalion 'opened on the enemy's batteries, and continued the cannonade until about dark.' A correspondent in the target area wrote: 'Then came a storm of shot and shell; marble slabs were broken, iron fences shattered, horses disembowelled.'

Meanwhile, Lieutenant-Colonel William Nelson's battalion remained in reserve. It did not fire a shot for the whole of July 2.

II Army Corps Reserve Artillery
Colonel John Thompson Brown
4 Staff and Field Officers

1st Virginia Artillery Battalion
Captain Willis Jefferson Dance
9 Staff and Field Officers

2nd Company Richmond Howitzers (Virginia)
Captain David Watson
4 x 10-pounder Parrott rifled guns
(64 troops present for duty equipped)

3rd Company Richmond Howitzers (Virginia)
Captain Benjamin Hodges Smith, Jr.
4 x 3-inch rifled guns
(62 troops present for duty equipped)

1st Rockbridge Artillery (Virginia)
Captain Archibald Graham
4 x 20-pounder Parrott rifled guns
(85 troops present for duty equipped)

Powhatan Artillery (Virginia)
Lieutenant John M. Cunningham
4 x 3-inch rifled guns
(78 troops present for duty equipped)

Salem Flying Artillery (Virginia)
Lieutenant Charles Beale Griffin
2 x 3-inch rifled guns
2 x 12-pounder Napoleon guns
(69 troops present for duty equipped)

Nelson's Battalion of Artillery
Lieutenant-Colonel William Nelson
9 Staff and Field Officers

Amherst Artillery (Virginia)
Captain Thomas Jellis Kirkpartick
1 x 3-inch rifled gun
3 x 12-pounder Napoleon guns
(105 troops present for duty equipped)

Fluvanna Artillery (Virginia)
Captain John Livingston Massie
1 x 3-inch rifled gun
3 x 12-pounder Napoleon guns
(90 troops present for duty equipped)

Georgia Regular Battery
Captain John Milledge, Jr.
2 x 3-inch rifled guns
1 x 10-pounder Parrott rifled gun
(73 troops present for duty equipped)

ARMY OF NORTHERN VIRGINIA II CORPS' BATTLES

Johnson's Division

Culp's Hill – A Failure of Timing – 1600–2200 hrs

Lee's plan called for Ewell's Corps to make a demonstration in support of Longstreet's flank attack. It was 'to be converted into a real attack if an opportunity offered.' It was to start at about 1600 hrs and to involve the entire corps. Johnson's Division would attack Culp's Hill. When Early and Rodes heard that Johnson was engaged, they would assault Cemetery Hill.

Early in the morning, 19-year-old Major Joseph Latimer searched for artillery positions to support Johnson's infantry attack. The best available was Benner's Hill. It overlooked Gettysburg from astride the Hanover Road. From its bare crest, artillery could fire about 1,000 yards to Culp's Hill and 1,500 yards to East Cemetery Hill. The four-gun Rockbridge Artillery occupied a hilltop position north of the Hanover Road. Latimer's Battalion, with 16 tubes, would unlimber 200 yards away along the open crest when the signal came.

When he heard the sounds of Longstreet's fight, General Johnson ordered Latimer to 'open fire with all his pieces' shortly after 1600 hrs. Latimer, 'the Boy Major' complied. Hardly had the first Confederate shot

Late in the afternoon Latimer's artillery battalion deployed on Benner's Hill to bombard Culp's Hill in preparation for the infantry attack. In the gathering dusk, Johnson's Division made its doomed assault.

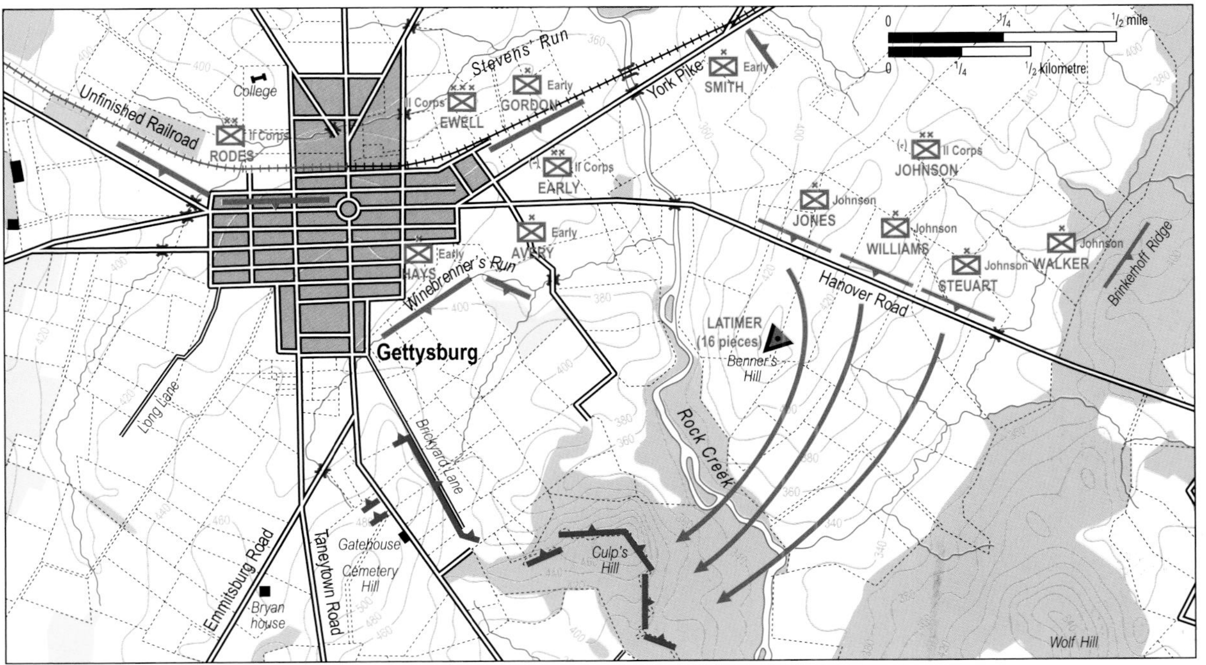

1200 hrs	1300	1400	1500	1600	1700	1800	1900	2000	2100	2200
pages 30-31				32-39	40-43	91-93		70-73		

been fired before the Federal guns on Culp's Hill responded. A Maryland gunner recalls, 'Benner's Hill was simply a hell infernal.' When Latimer realised that the hostile fire was ruining his battalion, he informed Johnson that he could not remain in place. Johnson instructed him to withdraw but to leave four pieces on the hill to support the pending infantry charge. These four guns attracted 'a terrible fire.' Among the battalion's 10 killed and 40 wounded was Latimer, who received a mortal wound. The rebel bombardment of Culp's Hill failed to prepare the way for the infantry.

Culp's Hill comprised two peaks. The highest stood 180 feet above Rock Creek, which ran along its eastern face. Four hundred yards to the south and 100 feet lower was a second peak. A seven-acre cleared field, now called 'Pardee Field', crowned the lower slope. To attack this position, the rebels would have to ford Rock Creek and make a steep climb up through a heavily wooded, boulder-strewn slope.

The second of July was an anxious day of waiting for Johnson's men. They well knew that the defenders were 'plying axe and pick and shovel in fortifying a position which was already sufficiently formidable.' The Stonewall Brigade was detached to provide flank security. It had orders to repulse the Union cavalry on Brinkerhoff's Ridge and then join the division as soon as possible.

The three remaining brigades numbered about 4,000 men. Because of a Union error, they confronted only a single, 1,350-man brigade commanded by Brigadier-General Greene atop the hill. At 1900 hrs the infantry charged.

From the beginning it was apparent that the soldiers had no notion that they were merely ordered to create a diversion. Instead they tried to capture the heights at bayonet point. Jones' Brigade attacked Greene's left, Nicholls' Louisiana Brigade, led by Colonel Jesse Milton, Greene's centre, and Steuart's Brigade Greene's right. Jones' Virginians had little chance. It was dark in the woods and their line be-came jumbled. When they neared the Union breastworks they received a punishing musketry fire. 'All was confusion and disorder' recalled a Virginian. A private remembered the yankee position as 'a ditch filled with men firing down on our heads.' They charged three times but did not come close to carrying the position. Among the casualties was General Jones, who received a nasty thigh wound.

Williams' Louisianians fared no better. They climbed 'as best they could up the steep hill side over rocks and through the timber up to the enemy's line of works.' The brigade recoiled and engaged in a desultory firefight at about 100 yards range until the end of the battle.

Because of the terrain, Steuart's two right-hand units, the 3rd North Carolina and 1st Maryland Battalion, made fast progress during the approach march. They were unfortunate because they entered the open side of an inverted V-shaped defence. Thus they received fire from front and flank. Their line 'reeled and staggered like a drunken man.' Meanwhile, the rest of the brigade passed beyond Greene's flank, occupied some vacated works, and wheeled across the Pardee Field to strike Greene's right.

Steuart sent one of his aides to guide the 1st North Carolina from his own left flank to assist his embattled right. The aide led them up a draw until he came abreast of a line of muzzle flashes. He also saw firing to his front. He ordered the 1st to deploy and fire to its front. Unfortunately, they were shooting at the brigade's own 1st Maryland.

Although stalled on its right, Steuart's Brigade con-

The fighting was so intense that four years later a visitor to the north-east slopes of Culp's Hill found the trees 'completely riddled' by musketry with most of the largest girdled and dead from the shock. (MOLLUS)

1200 hrs	1300	1400	1500	1600	1700	1800	1900	2000	2100	2200
pages 30-31				32-39	40-43	91-93		70-73		

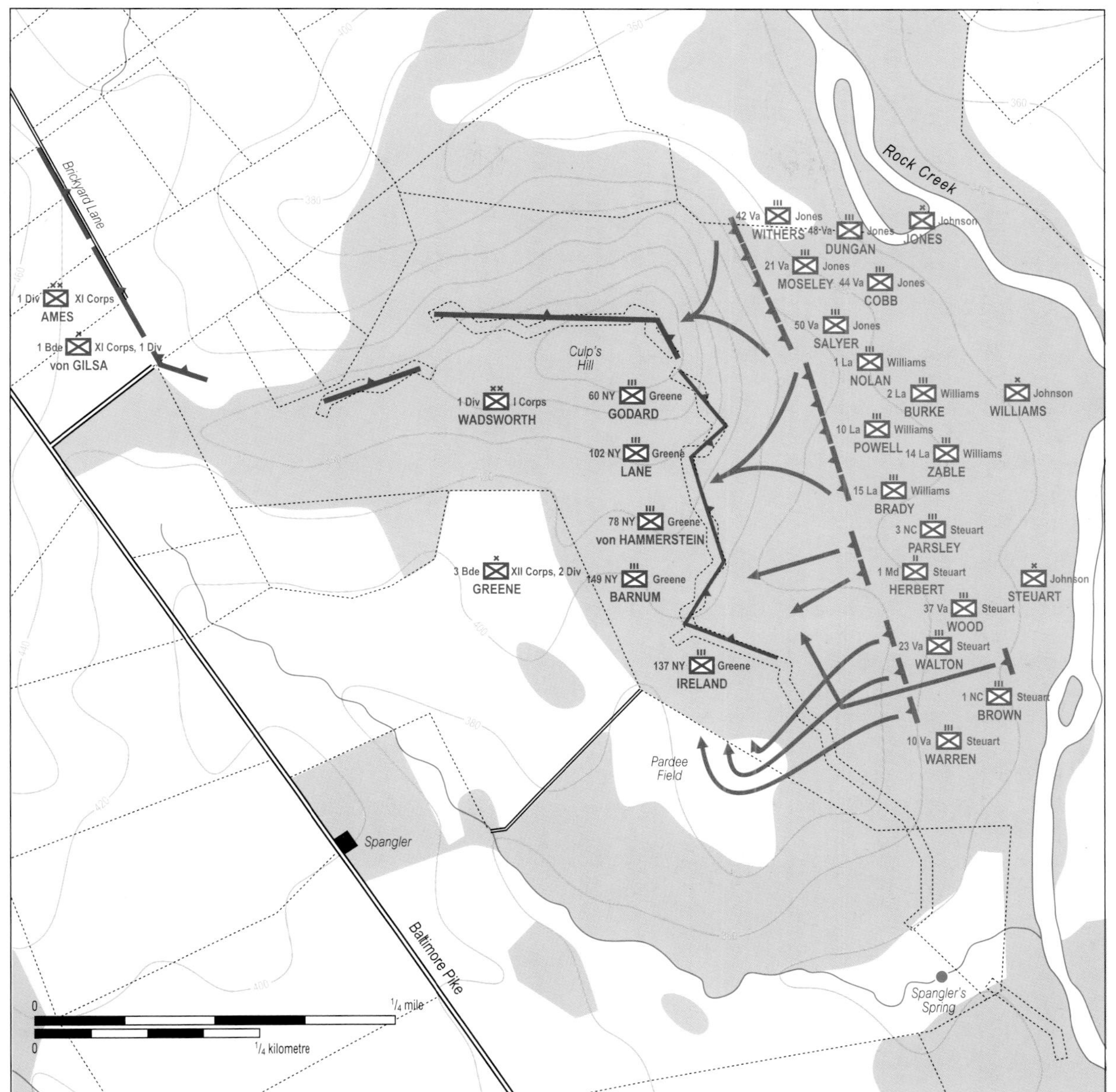

Because of a Federal blunder, Johnson's men were able to turn the enemy's flank and occupy the unmanned breastworks on the lower summit of Culp's Hill.

tinued to make progress on its left. Because of the darkness and battle smoke, it was hard to know where stood the enemy. Lieutenant-Colonel Walton of the 23rd Virginia sent a volunteer forward to locate the yankee line. The volunteer closed to within 20 paces of a unit, saw that they were the enemy, fired his pistol, and ran back to report to Walton. Rather than await orders, Walton resolved to 'charge the works if I lose every man in my regiment.'

The confusing and, from a Confederate perspective, unnecessary action at Culp's Hill ended around 2200 hrs. All the rebels had managed was to occupy an abandoned line of enemy works on the lower crest of the hill.

1200 hrs	1300	1400	1500	1600	1700	1800	1900	2000	2100	2200
pages 30-31				32-39	40-43	91-93		70-73		

ARMY OF NORTHERN VIRGINIA II CORPS' BATTLES

Early's Division

The Fight for Cemetery Hill – 2000–2100 hrs

According to orders, the divisions of Early and Rodes were to attack Cemetery Hill after Johnson began his assault. Initially only two of Early's brigades were in suitable jump-off positions. Hays' Brigade was behind a small creek, Winebrenner's Run, just east of town. Beyond Hays' left flank was Hoke's Brigade commanded by Colonel Isaac Avery. These two brigades constituted only eight of Early's 17 regiments.

To prepare for the attack, Early summoned Gordon's Brigade from its blocking position east of Gettysburg on the York Pike. Gordon moved to the railroad east of Gettysburg where he occupied a position about a quarter mile behind the front line. But Early allowed Smith's Brigade to maintain its position on the York Pike in order to protect the corps' left rear. Normally the cavalry would have performed this duty.

Rodes' Division was less ready. His brigades lay scattered from positions behind the Seminary, along the railroad cut, and into Gettysburg where three brigades stretched along west Middle Street in the heart of town. Possibly because he did not want to expose his men to artillery fire, Rodes did not advance his units to an assault position before Early charged.

Unlike Culp's Hill, Cemetery Hill was not wooded. It also featured a more gentle slope. The area south of Gettysburg had numerous houses and outbuildings including two tanyards and a brickyard. Thus, a Confederate assault would have to come from the northeast and northwest of the hill. Numerous fences bisected the fields across which the attackers would march. Overall, Cemetery Hill was a weaker natural position than Culp's Hill and Confederate artillery could, in theory, provide converging fire against the former. The 20-pounder Parrotts of the Rockbridge Artillery could hit East Cemetery Hill, while Dance's Battalion with 12 tubes, and another 41 tubes from Hill's Corps were in position to strike the crest of Cemetery Hill. However the yankees packed 43 artillery pieces onto the hill. Events would show the Confederate artillery unable to dislodge them before the infantry assaulted.

During the day, rebel and yankee sharpshooters duelled among the buildings and fence lines north of Cemetery Hill. The fire was fierce and it kept soldiers on both sides pinned to their positions. After an ineffectual artillery bombardment, Early's two front-line assault brigades prepared to advance. When Early heard Johnson's Division charge, the roar of its fight sounded 'like that of a sea lashed in fury'. He rode to the front and ordered Brigadier-General Harry Hays to 'carry the works on the heights in their front.' Just as was the case at Culp's Hill, this order was a far cry from Lee's intention merely to create a diversion in favour of Longstreet.

Hays' five Louisiana regiments numbered about 1,200 men. Because the brigade had to conduct a wheel to strike the Federal line, it was difficult for the advancing regiments to maintain contact. Hays' two farthest right-hand regiments hit the short side of the Union L-shaped position at the base of the hill before the remainder of the brigade made contact. These regiments, probably the 5th and 6th Louisiana, encountered musketry from the defenders behind a fence line. An eyewitness related, 'They moved forward steadily, amid this hail of shot and minnie ball, as though they were on parade far removed from danger.' The defenders faltered and retreated up the hill toward their supporting batteries.

The balance of Hays' Brigade completed its wheel and advanced against the long side of the L-shaped defence. Avery's three regiments, with about 900 men, initially moved forward on Hays' left. But the front narrowed as they advanced, so in all likelihood the

1200 hrs	1300	1400	1500	1600	1700	1800	1900	2000	2100	2200
pages 30-31				32-39,67-69	40-43	91-93				

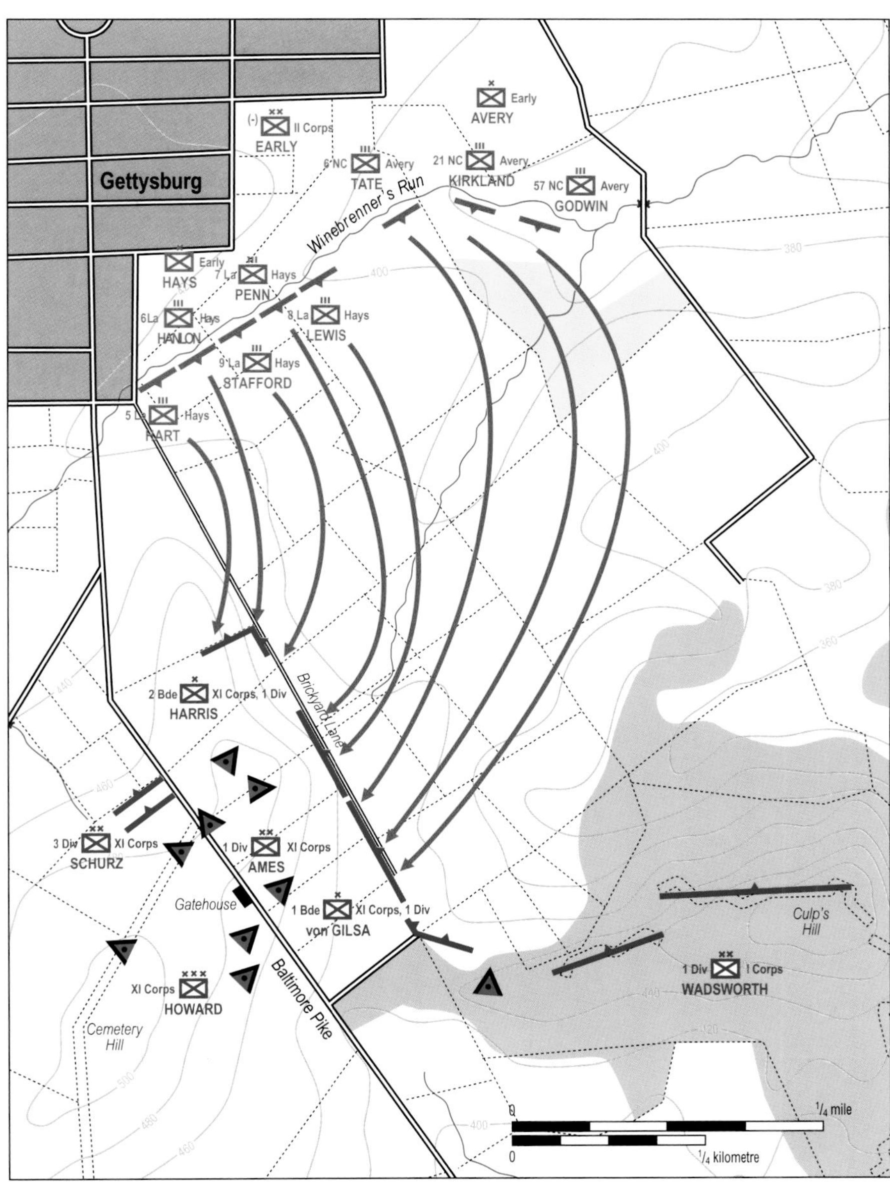

When Early heard Johnson's Division attack Culp's Hill, he ordered two brigades to advance against Cemetery Hill. The Federal positions there had been improved all day, with a formidable gun line of 43 pieces to the rear.

Confederates formed two lines. These lines had to endure artillery fire from their front as well as enfilading fire from the saddle of ground connecting Cemetery Hill with Culp's Hill. The fences proved more of an obstacle than anticipated. Colonel Archibald Godwin wrote that three fence lines and the uneven ground 'prevented that rapidity of movement and unity of action which might have insured success.'

Along most of the long side of the 'L', the Confederates also encountered fierce musketry. Against this fire they made little progress. Unnoticed among the casualties at the time was the loss of Colonel Avery. He received a mortal wound. As he lay dying, he scrawled a last message: 'Tell my father I died with my face to the enemy.'

A Union blunder had left a hole in their line. Into this gap pressed a handful of North Carolina soldiers from Avery's Brigade. Adjacent to the gap occurred brief hand to hand combat. Colonel Godwin deflected a clubbed musket with his left arm and then slew his foe

1200 hrs	1300	1400	1500	1600	1700	1800	1900	2000	2100	2200
pages 30-31				32-39,67-69	40-43	91-93				

with his sword-wielding right arm. As the rebels widened the breach, nearby Union soldiers began to break and run uphill. At considerable cost, Early's two assault brigades had managed to punch two holes in the Union infantry line defending the base of Cemetery Hill. According to a North Carolina major, only about 75 of his soldiers and perhaps a dozen Louisianians exploited the gap in the long side of the Union 'L'-shaped defence. In the darkness they climbed toward Rickett's Battery on the crest. Likewise, a narrow column belonging to Hays' right wing ascended toward Wiedrich's Battery on the northern tip of Cemetery Hill. The remainder of the two brigades struggled to reform at the base of the hill.

The brigades of Hays and Avery made two partial breakthroughs on Cemetery Hill but were forced to retire. Gordon's Brigade should have advanced to support them from the north with Rodes' Division attacking from the west.

The rebels swarmed around both batteries. Some Louisiana soldiers, 'yelling like demons', briefly held some cannons but they were too few to retain the guns. A brief but furious point-blank combat ensued. A Federal lieutenant and a Louisiana colour-bearer grappled for the flag of the 8th Louisiana. A rebel l ieutenant seized a battery guidon. The guidon bearer pistolled the lieutenant, seized the guidon, and then received a mortal wound himself. Nearby, a rebel pointed his rifle and demanded the battery surrender. A Union sergeant knocked him to the ground with a rock.

The Confederates sent for reinforcements. Instead, they heard and then saw an unknown mass of men

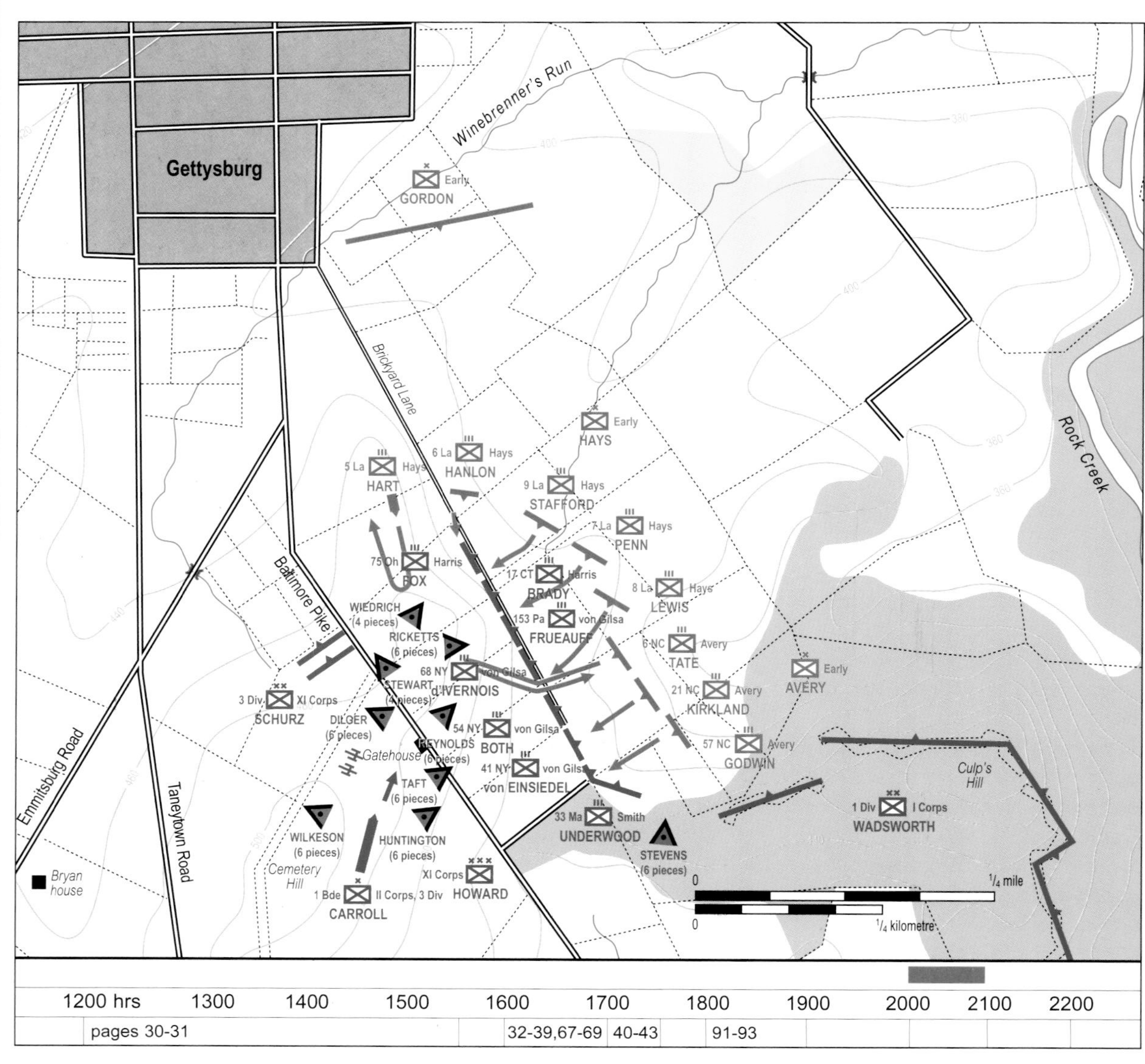

moving toward them from the cemetery. Because they expected help from Rodes' Division, Hays ordered his men to hold their fire. The unknown line fired a volley and approached nearer. It fired a second, and then a third volley. Only then, by the light of their muzzle flashes, could the rebels see that they faced a fresh Federal force. Hays ordered his men to return the fire and it seemed to check temporarily the yankees. But Hays saw that several more enemy lines were following. He ordered his men to fall back to the base of the hill. This ended one Confederate penetration.

At the other, the commanding major managed twice to repel Union counter-attacks. Then the absence of support compelled him also to order a retreat. As a survivor ruefully described the situation, it was 'a success that did not succeed.'

When the first two brigades had charged, General Early ordered Gordon's Brigade to advance. This took longer than expected and by the time Gordon de-ployed along Winebrenner's Run, an officer on Early's staff could see Hays' and Avery's 'line rolling rapidly up the hill'.

It was what Early did not see that worried him. Rodes' Division had not yet moved forward. Early concluded that in the absence of support from Rodes, ordering Gordon forward would be 'a useless sacrifice.' Thus, when Hays went searching for support, he discovered Gordon's men inert, occupying the same start line that his own brigade had occupied before it charged. Then and thereafter he was furious.

Rodes had kept his division in its sheltered position until Longstreet's attack began and he saw enemy soldiers moving on Cemetery Hill. Rather than order his own men to advance, he went to confer first with Early and then with someone in Pender's Division. Why he had not earlier coordinated with the two adjacent divisions remains a mystery. When he finally ordered his men to move to their start line, he discovered that extricating three brigades from Gettysburg's streets was more time consuming than anticipated.

The division formed with three brigades forward along Long Lane and two brigades in a supporting line. Then Rodes made the unusual decision to have the entire force conform to his front right-hand brigade commanded by Brigadier-General Stephen Dodson Ramseur. Ramseur's North Carolinians moved forward toward Cemetery Hill oppressed by a sense of doom. They had seen that the objective was packed with artillery and defended by infantry deployed behind

The gate building to the Evergreen Cemetery, named after the pine trees that grew atop Cemetery Hill. (MOLLUS)

stone walls. They believed that they marched to certain destruction.

Ramseur apparently agreed. He halted his brigade a short way beyond Long Lane and went ahead to scout. Why this was necessary is another mystery.The objective had been in plain view during the day and it was unlikely that Ramseur could learn anything useful by conducting a moonlit reconnaissance. In all likelihood, he was searching for a face-saving reason to call off the attack. Ramseur reported that he saw batteries 'in position to pour upon our lines direct, cross, and enfilade fires' supported by two lines of infantry behind walls and breastworks. He returned to confer with his Generals Doles and Iverson. All agreed that it was pointless to attack.

Early's two brigades that did attack each lost about 300 men. They, like so many other Confederates on this day, believed that they had conducted a gallant assault, stood on the verge of success, and someone had erred by not supporting them. Later it could be seen that failure had occurred in part because the Confederate leaders, operating on exterior lines, were unable to coordinate their efforts and to reinforce their success.

1200 hrs	1300	1400	1500	1600	1700	1800	1900	2000	2100	2200
pages 30-31				32-39,67-69	40-43	91-93				

THE ARMY OF NORTHERN VIRGINIA

III CORPS

Five o'clock in the morning on July 2 found Lieutenant-General Ambrose Hill attending an informal conference on Seminary Ridge. Present were Lee, Longstreet, Hood and Heth. Hill listened while Longstreet, an officer whom he heartily disliked, objected to Lee's plan for an offensive. Lee insisted that Longstreet move his two available divisions to the army's right in order to strike the Union flank. Hill contributed little to the discussion beyond noting that the attack should occur early in the day in order to have enough daylight hours to capitalise on the anticipated victory. Clearly Hill understood that the army's partial success on July 1 stemmed in part from the late hour at which the final Confederate attacks had begun.

III CORPS

Lieutenant-General Ambrose Powell Hill

15 Staff and Field Officers

Anderson's Division
Major-General Richard Heron Anderson
Heth's Division
Brigadier-General James Johnston Pettigrew
Pender's Division
Major-General William Dorsey Pender/
Brigadier-General James Henry Lane
III Corps Reserve Artillery
Colonel Reuben Lindsay Walker

Both Heth's and Pender's Divisions of Lieutenant-General Ambrose Powell Hill's III Corps had been badly mauled during the fighting west of Gettysburg on July 1. On July 2 only Anderson's fresh division joined the Confederate attack on the Federal positions along the Emmitsburg Road. **(Carl Smith, Manassas)**

Hill's III Corps occupied the centre of the army's 5 1/2 -mile long line. The previous day, Heth's and Pender's Divisions had lost 2,836 infantry killed or wounded with another 1,030 missing or captured. Anderson's fresh division, which had arrived on Herr Ridge around 1700 hrs on July 1, stretched along Seminary Ridge with its right flank resting on Pitzer's Woods. Until Longstreet's Corps marched, Anderson's men guarded the army's right flank. Pender's Division continued the line along the ridge all of the way to the Hagerstown Road. Two of the division's brigades had suffered severe losses on the previous day, but the division was in good spirits. Heth's battered division stayed in reserve.

Garnett's and McIntosh's artillery battalions deployed along Seminary Ridge on the corps' left between the McMillan House and the Hagerstown Road. Pegram's Battalion deployed on the ridge in front of McMillan's Woods. Lane's Battalion was on the right of the corps' line.

Hill understood that Lee intended his corps to assist Longstreet. Exactly how he was to accomplish this remains murky. Hill later reported, 'I was ordered to co-operate with him with such of my brigades from the right as could join in with his troops in the attack.' Lee later wrote that Hill 'was instructed to threaten the centre of the Federal line, in order to prevent reinforcements being sent to either wing' and to attack if the opportunity arose. Yet hours after Hill knew what was expected of his corps, Anderson remained ignorant of his role. Then, when Anderson learned about Longstreet's pending flank attack, he reported that his orders required him to attack by brigade, or in echelon, once Longstreet progressed to the point that his corps was in close contact with Anderson's right. Yet the commander of Anderson's right-hand brigade, Brigadier-General Cadmus Wilcox, denied ever having received an order to move in echelon.

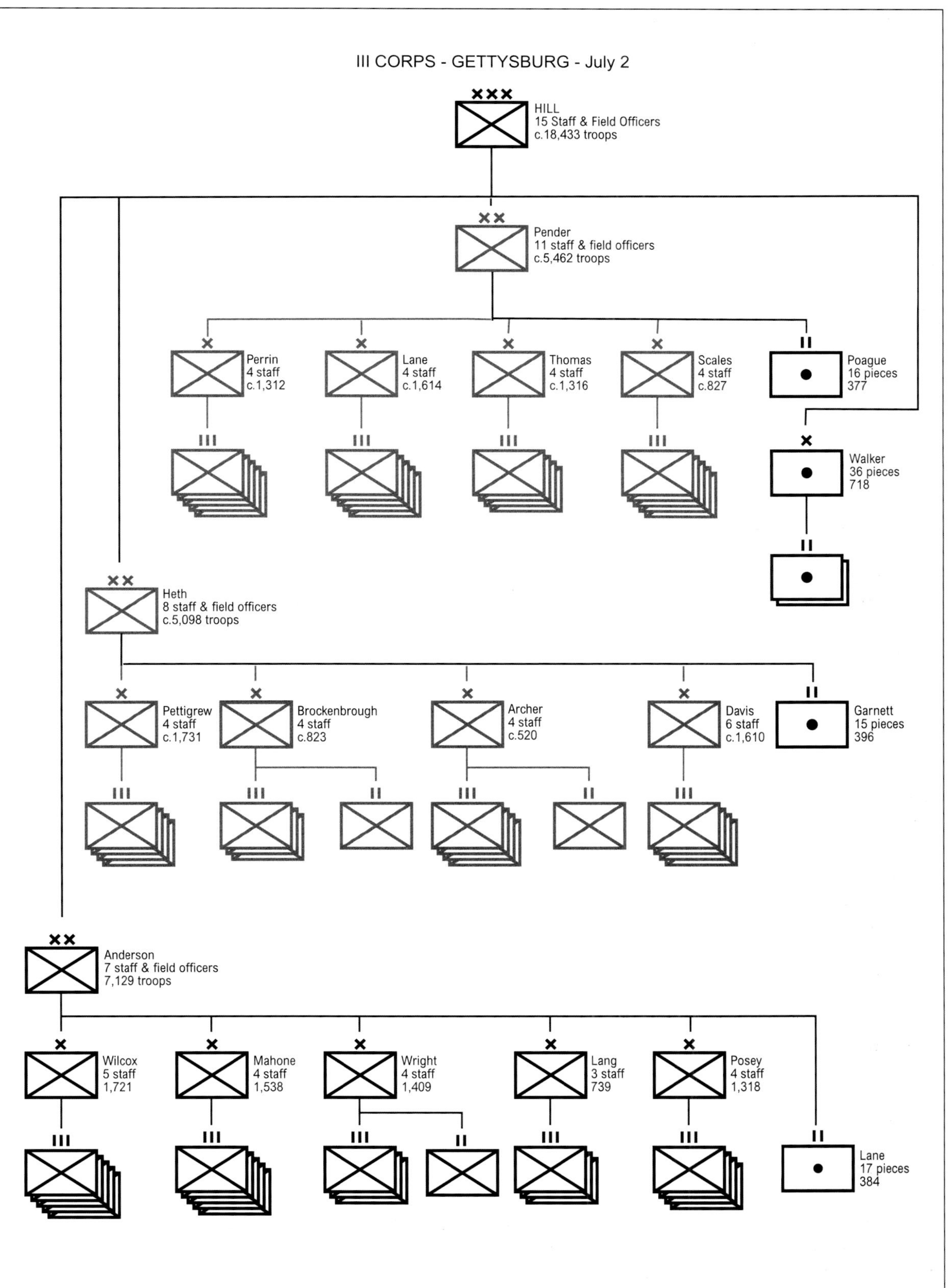

III CORPS - GETTYSBURG - July 2
HILL
15 Staff & Field Officers
c.18,433 troops
Pender
11 staff & field officers
c.5,462 troops
Perrin
4 staff
c.1,312
Lane
4 staff
c.1,614
Thomas
4 staff
c.1,316
Scales
4 staff
c.827
Poague
16 pieces
377
Walker
36 pieces
718
Heth
8 staff & field officers
c.5,098 troops
Pettigrew
4 staff
c.1,731
Brockenbrough
4 staff
c.823
Archer
4 staff
c.520
Davis
6 staff
c.1,610
Garnett
15 pieces
396
Anderson
7 staff & field officers
7,129 troops
Wilcox
5 staff
1,721
Mahone
4 staff
1,538
Wright
4 staff
1,409
Lang
3 staff
739
Posey
4 staff
1,318
Lane
17 pieces
384

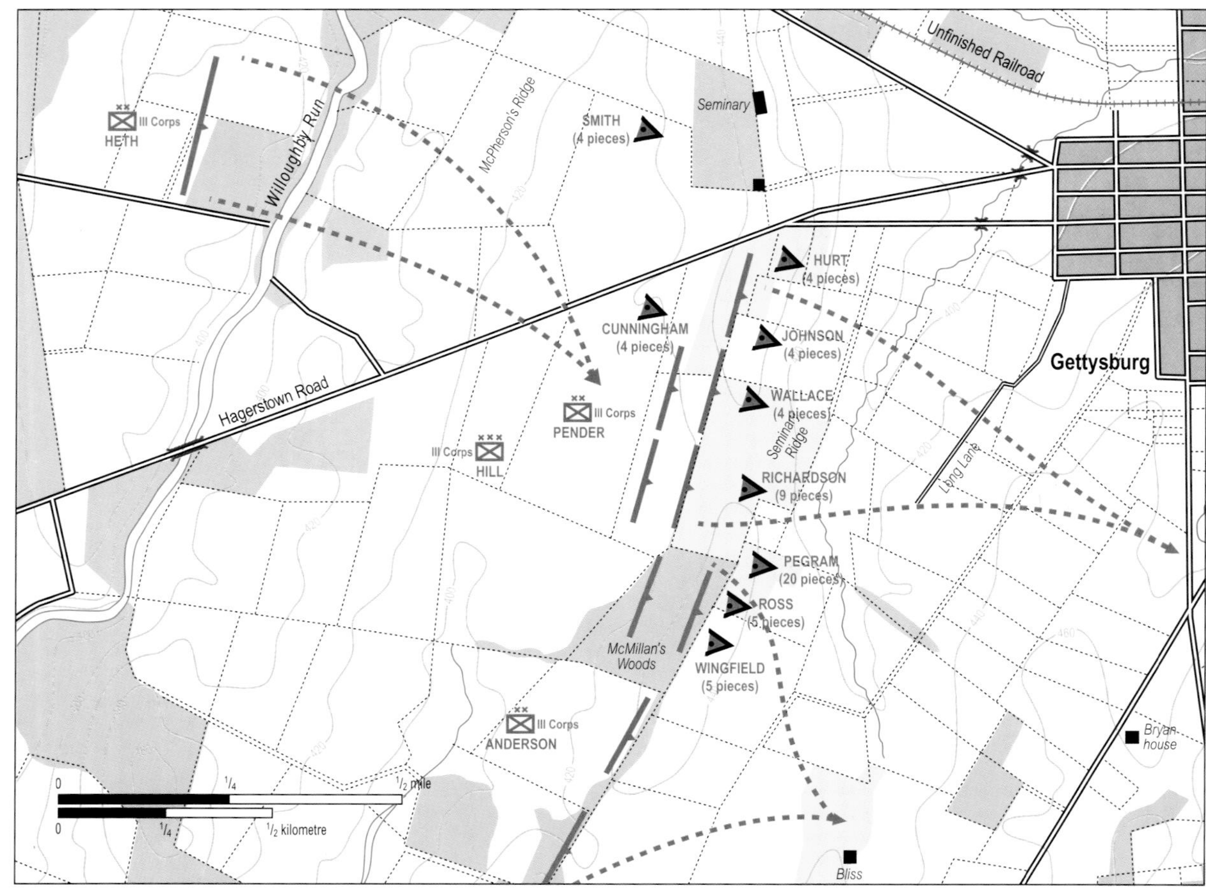

Hill's III Corps, with Heth's battered division to the rear, was deployed to exploit a collapse of either of the Federal wings. III Corps primary task was to assist Longstreet if he succeeded in rolling up the Union left flank. It could also be thrown against the north end of Cemetery Ridge if a breakthrough occured there.

Clearly something was amiss in III Corps' chain of command. This may have stemmed from Hill's recurring illness. An observer wrote that Hill appeared 'very delicate' the evening before. Hill's inexperience at corps' command contributed to the muddle as perhaps did his lack of familiarity with his subordinate, Anderson. Lee's command style was to devise a plan and allow his corps' commanders to execute it. This worked well when Stonewall Jackson was alive. It failed with Hill at Gettysburg.

Hill established his headquarters at the Emanuel Pitzer farmhouse behind the centre of his line. For most of the day he was either with or near Lee so there should have been no confusion. Lee probably sensed that Hill was not behaving in the competent, aggressive style that had earned him army-wide accolades. Accordingly, before Longstreet engaged, Lee rode to Wilcox to deliver instructions personally. His uncharacteristic behaviour is suggestive. Colonel Edward Porter Alexander related that there was never 'any conference or discussions among our generals at this time as to the best formations and tactics in making our attack.' Given what was to occur, this omission was hugely significant.

Prior to Longstreet's attack, Hill ordered his Chief of Artillery, Colonel R. Lindsay Walker, to stay alert and to support Longstreet whenever possible. Walker's adjutant, in turn, showed the order to the artillery battalion commanders. They, at least, were fully briefed and prepared.

III Corps Casualties at Gettysburg
July 2, 1863

Infantry killed or wounded 991
Infantry missing/captured 667
Artillery killed or wounded 66
Artillery missing/captured 3

III Corps – Anderson's Division

After an 18-mile march, Anderson's Division arrived on Herr's Ridge via the Chambersburg Pike on July 1 at around 1700 hrs. Lee elected to retain the division in reserve for the rest of the day.

During the morning of July 2, Hill ordered the division forward to Seminary Ridge to occupy a position on Pender's right flank. The deployment along a mile-long front was complete around noon. Wilcox had a 'sharp skirmish' with a Federal scouting group in Pitzer's Woods but otherwise the division remained inactive. Sheltered in the trees, the men 'sweated, sweltered and swore' until 1800 hrs.

About 800 to 1,200 yards to the east, the men could plainly see the Union line on Cemetery Ridge. Lee's plan called for the division to attack towards the ridge once Longstreet's flank attack reached its front.

Major-General Richard Heron Anderson had brought his division 18 miles on July 1 to make it available for battle. However, Lee ordered the fresh division held in reserve. Anderson's time would come in the late afternoon of July 2. (MARS)

ANDERSON'S DIVISION
Major-General Richard Heron Anderson

Wilcox's Brigade - 1,721 troops
Mahone's Brigade - 1,538 troops
Wright's Brigade - 1,409 troops
Perry's (Lang's) Brigade - 739 troops
Posey's Brigade - 1,318 troops
Lane's Artillery Battalion - 375 troops

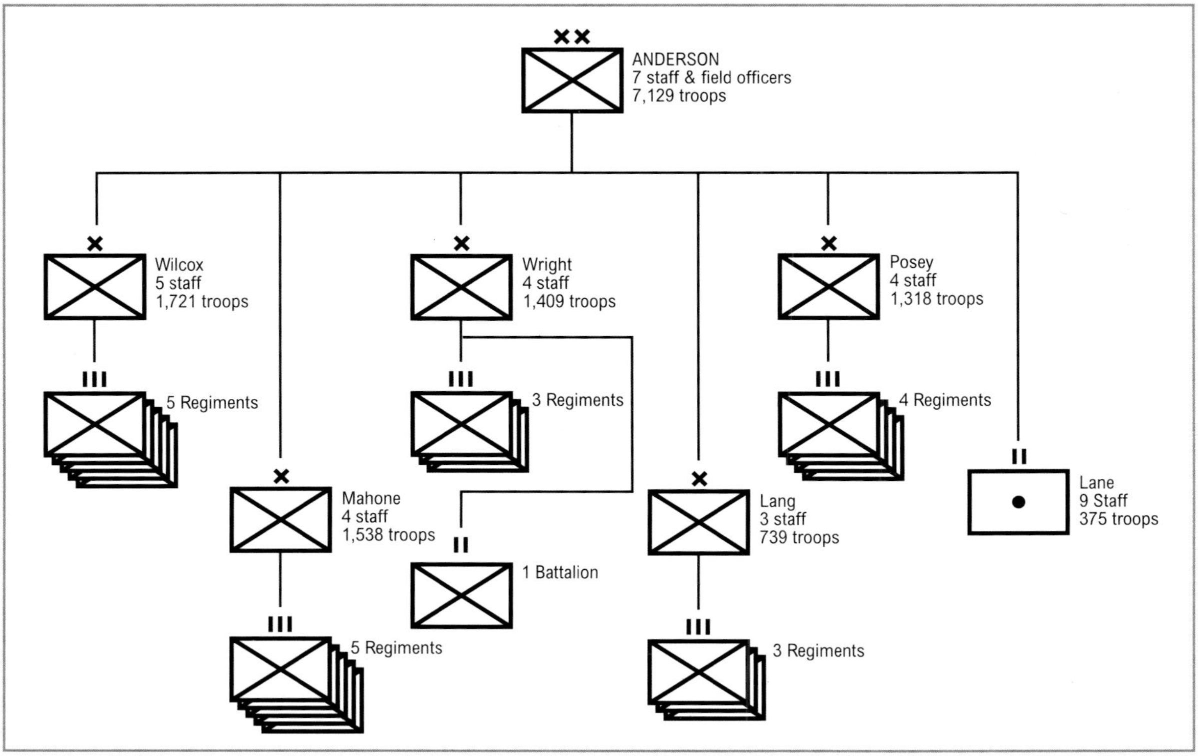

ANDERSON
7 staff & field officers
7,129 troops

Wilcox
5 staff
1,721 troops
5 Regiments

Mahone
4 staff
1,538 troops
5 Regiments

Wright
4 staff
1,409 troops
3 Regiments
1 Battalion

Lang
3 staff
739 troops
3 Regiments

Posey
4 staff
1,318 troops
4 Regiments

Lane
9 Staff
375 troops

Wilcox's Brigade

Wilcox's Brigade spent the night of July 1–2 on picket duty near Black Horse Tavern. At 0700 hrs on July 2 it rejoined the division. It marched south along Seminary Ridge to Pitzer's Woods. Here Major-General Anderson personally positioned the brigade in line with its right flank refused. The Federal picket line could be seen in front of Cemetery Ridge, about 600 to 700 yards away. Wilcox did not know if Pitzer's Woods, just in front of his right flank, were occupied. Accordingly, the 10th Alabama advanced to occupy the woods.

A stern skirmish ensued, described by Wilcox as very 'creditable to the Tenth Alabama and its gallant colonel'. By 0900 hrs the fight had ended. The 10th Alabama continued to face south with the remainder of the brigade facing Cemetery Ridge.

Beginning around 1400 hrs, the brigade saw

Brigadier-General Cadmus Marcellus Wilcox, despite having been passed over for promotion, led his brigade valiantly on July 2. The Alabama brigade took heavy losses while penetrating the enemy line on Cemetery Ridge. (MARS)

WILCOX'S BRIGADE
Brigadier-General Cadmus Marcellus Wilcox

8th Alabama Infantry Regiment
Lieutenant-Colonel Hilary Abner Herbert
9th Alabama Infantry Regiment
Colonel Joseph Horace King/
Successor's name not available
10th Alabama Infantry Regiment
Colonel William Henry Forney/
Lieutenant-Colonel James E. Shelley
11th Alabama Infantry Regiment
Colonel John Caldwell Calhoun Sanders
Lieutenant-Colonel George Edward Tayloe
14th Alabama Infantry Regiment
Colonel Lucius Pinckard/
Lieutenant-Colonel James Andrew Broome

8th Alabama Infantry Regiment

Co. A	Royston's Alabama Rangers
Co. B	Governor's Guards
Co. C	Alex Stephens' Guards
Co. D	Independent Blues
Co. E	Hamp Smith Rifles
Co. F	Captain Hilary A. Herbert's Co.
Co. G	Captain John P. Emrich's Co.
Co. H	Mobile Independent Scouts
Co. I	Emerald Guards
Co. K	Southern Guards

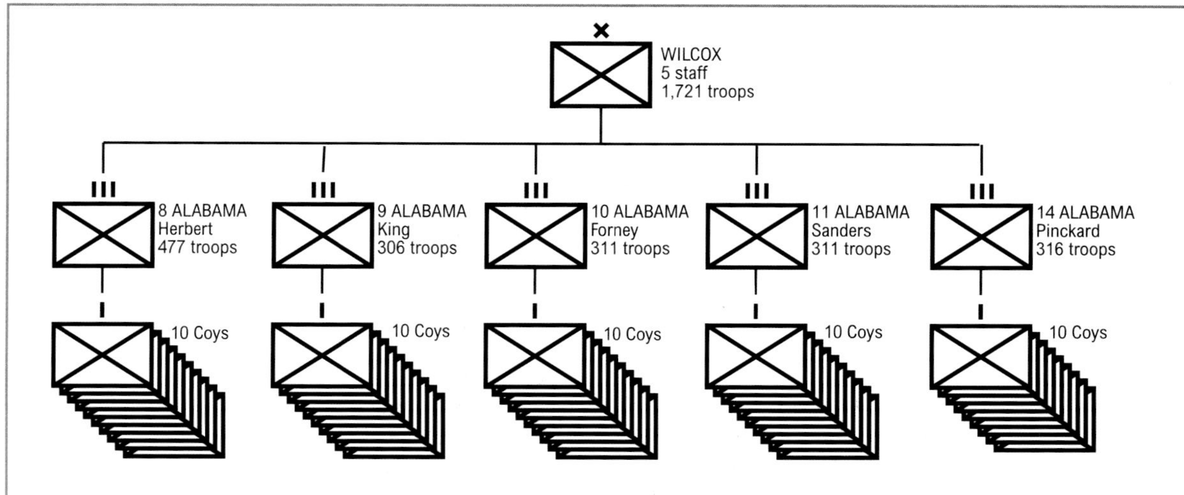

9th Alabama Infantry Regiment

Co. A	Beauregard Rifles
Co. B	Railroad Guards
Co. C	Pope Walker Guards
Co. D	Lauderdale Rifles
Co. E	Decatur Sons of Liberty
Co. F	Captain Thomas H. Hobbs' Co.
Co. G	Captain Edward Young Hill's Co.
Co. H	Limestone Grays
Co. I	Calhoun Guards
Co. K	Captain James L. Sheffield's Co.

11th Alabama Infantry Regiment

Co. A	Captain Young M. Moody's Co.
Co. B	Greene County Grays
Co. C	Confederate Guards
Co. D	Canebrake Legion
Co. E	Washington Sharpshooters
Co. F	Captain James L. Davidson's Co.
Co. G	North Port Rifles
Co. H	Pickens County Guards
Co. I	Captain George Traweek's Co.
Co. K	Captain Henry Talbird's Co.

McLaws' Division filing past its right flank to form at right angles to the brigade line. Wilcox reported, 'My instructions were to advance when the troops on my right should advance, and to report this to the division commander, in order that the other brigades should advance in proper time.' At about 1600 hrs a cannonade began. At 1820 hrs, Wilcox's troops saw McLaws begin to advance.

10th Alabama Infantry Regiment

Co. A	Ashville Guards
Co. B	Jefferson Volunteers
Co. C	Cahaba Valley Boys
Co. D	Alexandria Rifle Company
Co. E	Talladega Davis Blues
Co. F	Captain James D. Truss' Co.
Co. G	Pope Walker Guards
Co. H	Captain Woodford R. Hanna's Co.
Co. I	Captain Abner A. Hughes' Co.
Co. K	Captain John C. McKenzie's Co.

14th Alabama Infantry Regiment

Co. A	Captain William D. Harrington's Co.
Co. B	Captain James S. Williamson's Co.
Co. C	Captain Daniel H. McCoy's Co.
Co. D	Captain James A. Broome's Co.
Co. E	Captain William C. Allen's Co.
Co. F	Billy Gilmer Grays
Co. G	Hillabee Blues
Co. H	Jackson Avengers
Co. I	Talladega Hillabee Rifles
Co. K	Louisa Guards

Mahone's Brigade

The brigade camped on Herr Ridge on July 1. The next morning it marched along the Chambersburg Pike until filing south along Seminary Ridge. By noon it was in position on the division's far left where it faced east from McMillan's Woods. Its orders were to participate in the division's assault against Cemetery Ridge.

When the division's charge *en echelon* began, all proceeded well until Posey, the brigade commander who was to begin his attack just before Mahone, mishandled his unit and became bogged down in the fight for the Bliss Farm. Posey reported that he sent to Mahone for assistance, but that Mahone refused.

Mahone's conduct remains inexplicable. His terse

MAHONE'S BRIGADE
Brigadier-General William Mahone

6th Virginia Infantry Regiment
Colonel George Thomas Rogers
12th Virginia Infantry Regiment
Colonel David Addison Weisiger
16th Virginia Infantry Regiment
Colonel Joseph Hutchinson Ham
41st Virginia Infantry Regiment
Colonel William Allen Parham
61st Virginia Infantry Regiment
Colonel Virginius Despeaux Groner

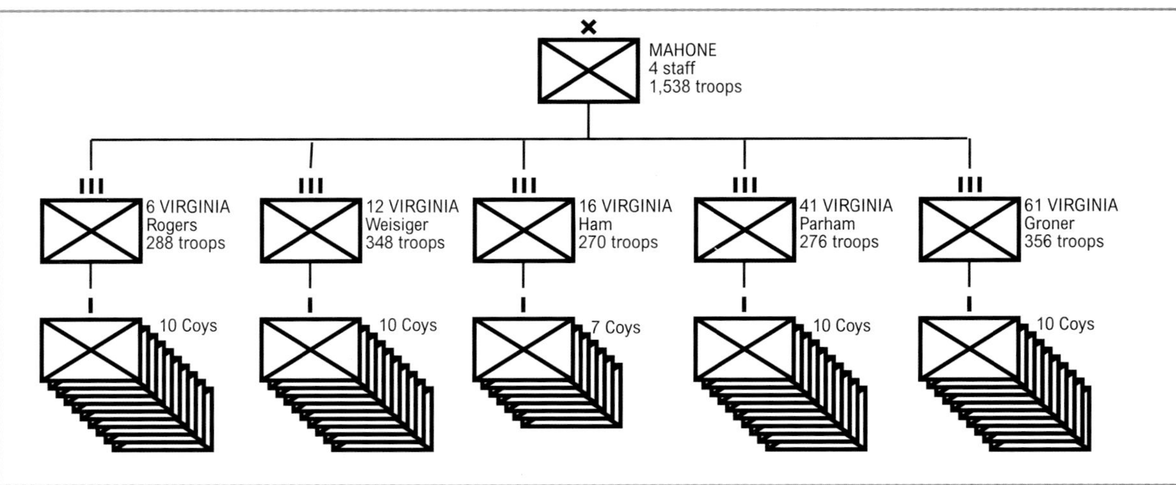

6th Virginia Infantry Regiment

Co. A	McKenney's Eyeteeth
Co. B	Princess Anne Grays
Co. C	Woodis Riflemen
Co. D	Norfolk Light Infantry
Co. E	Nansemond Guard
Co. F	Seaboard Rifles
Co. G	Southern Guard
Co. H	Independent Grays
Co. I	Elliott Grays
Co. K	Alstadt Grays

after action report fails to account for his inactivity. He wrote: 'The brigade took no special or active part in the actions of that battle [Gettysburg] beyond that which fell to the lot of its line of skirmishers.' Yet apparently, one of Anderson's aides rode to Mahone and delivered an order to advance. Mahone refused, commenting that Anderson had ordered him to remain in position. Afterwards, Mahone received much criticism from the Southern press. Anderson manfully diverted blame from his brigadiers and absorbed it himself.

12th Virginia Infantry Regiment

Co. A	Petersburg City Guard
Co. B	Petersburg Greys Co. A
Co. C	Petersburg Greys, Co. B
Co. D	Lafayette Guard
Co. E	Petersburg Rifles
Co. F	Huger Greys
Co. G	Richmond Grays
Co. H	Norfolk Juniors
Co. I	Captain Richard W. Jones' Co.
Co. K	Archer Rifles

16th Virginia Infantry Regiment

Co. A	Marion Rangers
Co. B	Suffolk Continentals
Co. C	Virginia Defenders
Co. D	Isle of Wight Rifle Grays
Co. E	Sussex Riflemen
Co. F	Fleet Rifle Guard
Co. G	Name not available

41st Virginia Infantry Regiment

Co. A	Sussex Sharpshooters
Co. B	Confederate Grays
Co. C	McRae Rifles
Co. D	Rough and Ready Volunteers
Co. E	Confederate Guards
Co. F	Norfolk County Rifle Patriots
Co. G	Ragland Guards
Co. H	Captain George E. Beaton's Co.
Co. I	Cypress Chapel Sharpshooters
Co. K	South Quay Guards

61st Virginia Infantry Regiment

Co. A	Jackson's Grays
Co. B	Wilson Guard
Co. C	Blanchard Greys
Co. D	Jackson Light Infantry
Co. E	Border Rifles
Co. F	Isle of Wight Avengers
Co. G	Confederate Defenders
Co. H	Virginia Rangers
Co. I	Bilisoly Blues
Co. K	Captain Maximillian Herbert's Co.

Wright's Brigade

Wright's Brigade was behind Mahone's Brigade during the July 1 march to Gettysburg. It was a start-stop-start march. Wright reported that although the men could hear the sounds of battle, the brigade remained motionless outside Cashtown for 60 to 90 minutes. The brigade resumed its march and arrived on Herr Ridge between 1600 and 1700 hrs.

Brigadier-General Ambrose Wright recovered from a 'severe indisposition' to reunite with his brigade on July 2 at 0700 hrs. He found the brigade in line of battle awaiting orders. Anderson instructed Wright to follow Perry's Brigade and to move by the right flank to a position along Seminary Ridge. Here it sheltered in a narrow strip of trees between McMillan's Woods and Spangler's Woods.

As Wright understood matters, the entire division would soon attack the enemy's lines, 'commencing on our right by Wilcox's brigade, and that each brigade of the division would begin the attack as soon as the

Brigadier-General Ambrose Ransom Wright, 37, had worked his way up from poverty to become a successful lawyer in Georgia. He fell ill on July 1 but returned to his command the next day. His brigade alone would reach the heights of Cemetery Ridge on July 2. (MARS)

WRIGHT'S BRIGADE
Brigadier-General Ambrose Ransom Wright/
Colonel William Gibson/
Brigadier-General Ambrose Ranson Wright

3rd Regiment Georgia Volunteer Infantry
Colonel Edward J. Walker
22nd Regiment Georgia Volunteer Infantry
Colonel Joseph Wasden/
Captain Benjamin C. McCurry
48th Regiment Georgia Volunteer Infantry
Colonel William Gibson/
Captain Matthew Robert Hall/
Colonel William Gibson
2nd Battalion Georgia Volunteer Infantry
Major George W. Ross/
Captain Charles J. Moffett/
Successor's name not available

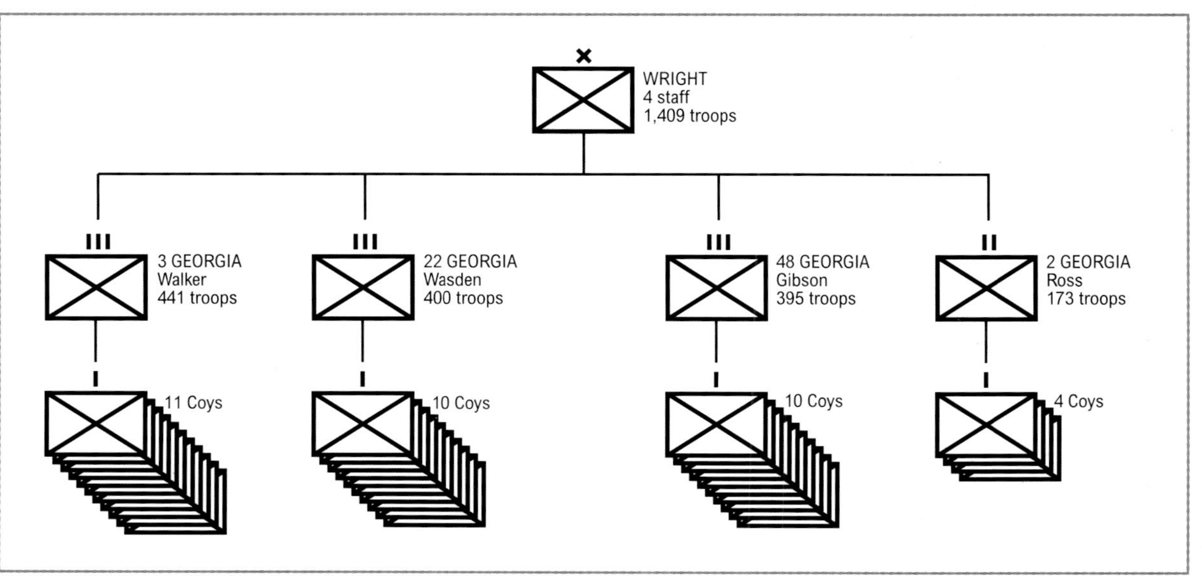

3rd Regiment Georgia Volunteer Infantry

Co. A	Burke Guards
Co. B	Brown Rifles
Co. C	Dawson Grays
Co. D	Home Guards
Co. E	Govenor Guards
Co. F	Wilkerson Rifles
Co. G	Confederate Light Guards
Co. H	Young Guard
Co. I	Blodget Volunteers
Co. K	Atlanta Guards
Co. L	Clarke County Rifles

22nd Regiment Georgia Volunteer Infantry

Co. A	Name not available
Co. B	Glascock Independent Guards
Co. C	Freeman Infantry
Co. D	Name not available
Co. E	Warsaw Rebels
Co. F	Bartow Volunteers
Co. G	Fireside Defenders
Co. H	Gardner Volunteers
Co. I	Name not available
Co. K	Henry Volunteers

48th Regiment Georgia Volunteer Infantry

Co. A	Gibson Volunteers
Co. B	Warren Infantry
Co. C	Georgia Light Infantry
Co. D	Burke Volunteers
Co. E	Jefferson Volunteers
Co. F	Battleground Guards
Co. G	Slappey Guards
Co. H	McLeod Volunteers
Co. I	Wilson Tigers
Co. K	Hamilton Rangers

brigade on its immediate right commenced the movement. I was instructed to move simultaneously with Perry's brigade, which was on my right, and informed that Posey's brigade, on my left, would move forward upon my advance.'

2nd Battalion Georgia Volunteer Infantry

Co. A	City Light Guards
Co. B	Macon Volunteers
Co. C	Floyd Rifles
Co. D	Spalding Greys

Perry's (Lang's) Brigade

The three small regiments that made up the Florida Brigade were rather like a stepchild within the family of the Army of Northern Virginia. At Sharpsburg, while fighting in Pryor's Brigade, the 2nd and 8th Florida had been mishandled in the fight along the Sunken Lane. The Florida Brigade came into being following a reorganisation after the Sharpsburg Campaign. The brigade's commander was Brigadier-General Edward Perry. Colonel David Lang, an officer who had risen from the rank of private in the 1st Florida, commanded the brigade's 8th Florida.

At Fredericksburg, the Floridians, together with Barksdale's Mississippi brigade, defended the river front against Federal efforts to bridge the Rappahannock River. Although the Mississippians garnered most of the glory, the Floridians acquitted themselves equally well. Among the 8th Florida's casualties was Colonel Lang, who received a severe head wound.

Under Perry's command, the brigade fought at Chancellorsville where it lost 21 killed and 88 wounded. Thereafter, Perry fell ill. The senior colonel, Lang, assumed command for the invasion of Pennsylvania.

PERRY'S (LANG'S) BRIGADE
Colonel David Lang

2nd Florida Infantry Regiment
Major Walter Raleigh Moore
5th Florida Infantry Regiment
Captain Richmond N. Gardner
8th Florida Infantry Regiment
Lieutenant-Colonel William Baya

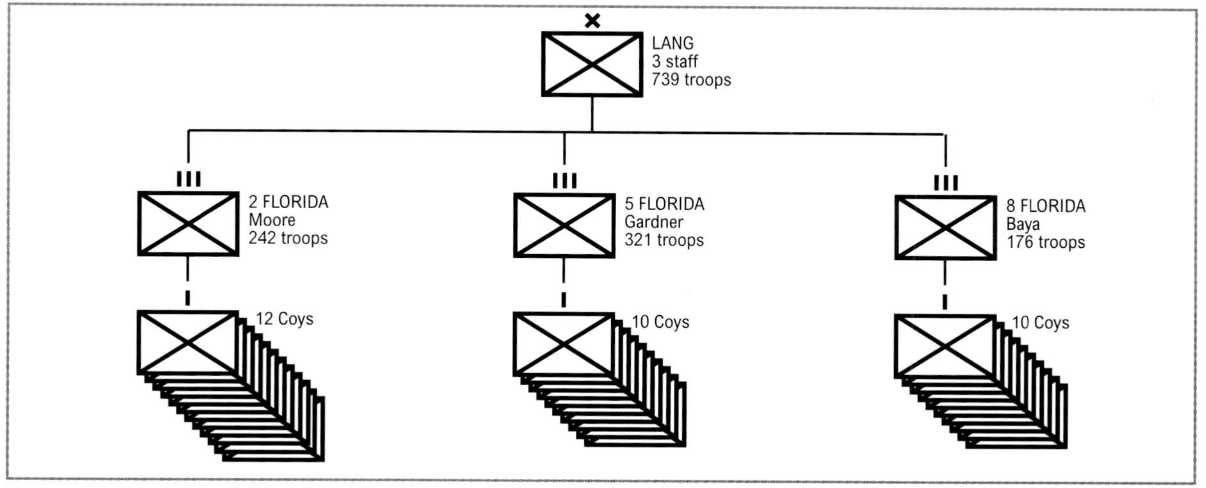

2nd Florida Infantry Regiment

Co. A	Rifle Rangers
Co. B	Name not available
Co. C	Columbia Rifles
Co. D	Florida Rangers
Co. E	Name not available
Co. F	Gulf State Guards
Co. G	Saint John's Greys
Co. H	Name not available
Co. I	Hamilton Blues
Co. K	Davis Guards
Co. L	Madison Rangers
Co. M	Howell Guards

5th Florida Infantry Regiment

Co. A	Milton Light Infantry
Co. B	Baker Guards
Co. C	Chapin Guards
Co. D	Bartow Rebels
Co. E	Madison Guerillas
Co. F	Frink Guards
Co. G	Anderson's Infantry
Co. H	Liberty Guards
Co. I	Wakulla Tigers
Co. K	Dixie Yeomen

Lang had participated in three battles, in two of them as a captain. His defence in the streets of Fredericksburg was a special case, a rare example of Civil War combat in a built-up area. Thus, although the 25-year old Lang was a graduate of the Georgia Military Institute, he otherwise had little formal military experience and no experience at all commanding a brigade in combat.

On July 1 the brigade formed the rear guard for Anderson's Division, marching to protect the divisional trains. When the sounds of battle came, Anderson ordered it to bypass the train and close up on the divisional column as it hastened towards Gettysburg. It camped on Herr Ridge, about two miles east of town.

During the morning of July 2, the brigade marched south along Seminary Ridge to a position facing east from Spangler's Woods. It occupied a fence that separated the woods from the open fields to the east. From left to right the order was: 2nd, 8th, and 5th Florida. On its right was Wilcox's Brigade, which, in the division's *en echelon* attack order, would begin the fight. On its left was Wright's Brigade. From this position, Lang could see the Federal troops on Cemetery Ridge, 'strongly entrenched in the woods and upon the heights.' In fact, the enemy was not entrenched. In front of Lang's men were several Union regiments along the Emmitsburg Road supported by a battery.

When Wilcox became involved in a skirmish in Pitzer's Woods, Lang's Brigade moved to assist the Alabamians. The Floridian's help was not needed so Lang returned to his original position. At this time his orders were to 'hold my position without bringing on an engagement unnecessarily until General Longstreet could come up on our right.'

At about 1700 hrs, Anderson sent an order announcing that Longstreet was driving the enemy and that Wilcox would advance when Longstreet's men approached his front. Anderson ordered Lang to advance his skirmish line and charge when Wilcox charged, 'holding all the ground the enemy yielded.'

8th Florida Infantry Regiment

Cos. A through K. All Company names not available.

Posey's Brigade

The veteran Mississippi soldiers of Posey's Brigade first fought under Posey's command at Chancellorsville. Posey had begun his association with the brigade when he organised a company in the 16th Mississippi and was then elected colonel. The 16th fought at Ball's Bluff, with Jackson during the Valley Campaign, and at Second Manassas and Sharpsburg. Thereafter Lee recommended Posey for promotion. During the Chancellorsville Campaign, both the brigade and its leader distinguished themselves.

Of all the Confederate brigades involved at Gettysburg, that of Brigadier-General Carnot Posey was to suffer the fewest casualties for the entire battle. (Museum of the Confederacy, Richmond)

POSEY'S BRIGADE
Brigadier-General Carnot Posey

12th Mississippi Volunteer Infantry Regiment
Colonel William H. Taylor
16th Mississippi Volunteer Infantry Regiment
Colonel Samuel E. Baker
19th Mississippi Volunteer Infantry Regiment
Colonel Nathaniel Harrison Harris
48th Mississippi Volunteer Infantry Regiment
Colonel Joseph McAfee Jayne

On July 2, 1863 the brigade marched south along Seminary Ridge and deployed amid the trees just

12th Mississippi Volunteer Infantry Regiment

Co. A	Clark Rifles
Co. B	Natchez Fencibles
Co. C	Raymond Fencibles
Co. D	Pettus Relief
Co. E	Sardis Blues
Co. F	Durant Rifles
Co. G	Vicksburg Sharpshooters
Co. H	Claiborne Guards
Co. I	Satartia Rifles
Co. K	Lawrence Rifles

16th Mississippi Volunteer Infantry Regiment

Co. A	Summit Rifles
Co. B	Name not available
Co. C	Crystal Springs Southern Rights
Co. D	Adams Light Guards No. 2
Co. E	Quitman Guards
Co. F	Jasper Greys
Co. G	Fairview Rifles
Co. H	Defenders
Co. I	Adams Light Guards No. 1
Co. K	Wilkinson Rifles

19th Mississippi Volunteer Infantry Regiment

Co. A	President Davis Guards
Co. B	Mott Guards
Co. C	Warren Rifles
Co. D	Thomas Hinds Guards
Co. E	McClung Riflemen
Co. F	Avent Southrons
Co. G	Springport Invincibles
Co. H	Name not available
Co. I	Name not available
Co. K	Jake Thompson Guards

48th Mississippi Volunteer Infantry Regiment

Co. A	Jackson Boys
Co. B	Rocky Point Rifles
Co. C	Name not available
Co. D	Dixie Boys
Co. E	Name not available
Co. F	Name not available
Co. G	Name not available
Co. H	Vicksburg Volunteers
Co. I	Wilkerson Guards
Co. L	Name not available

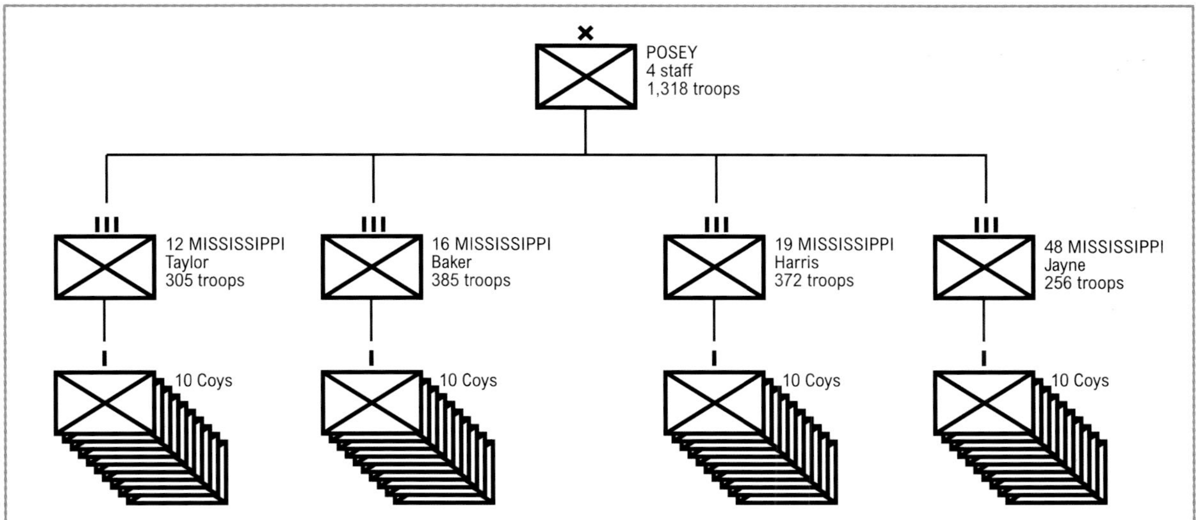

south of McMillan's Woods. The Union line on Cemetery Ridge was about 1,200 yards to the east.

Posey's orders were to advance when he saw the adjacent unit on his left, Wright's Brigade, begin its charge. Before that occurred, a new order came from the divisional commander to send two regiments forward to skirmish in front of the Bliss farm. In the event, the escalating combat for this farm absorbed too much of the brigade's strength and contributed to the mis-timed divisional assault.

Divisional Artillery – Sumter (Georgia) Artillery – 11th Georgia Battalion

The three Georgia batteries comprising the Sumter Battalion retained the old style designation as lettered companies rather than named batteries. The battalion arrived at Gettysburg around 1500 hrs on July 1 after a march without incident except for a few lame horses which had to be abandoned by the roadside.

Early on July 2, the corps' Chief of Artillery, Colonel Walker, ordered the battalion's commander, Major John Lane, to attach Company B to Wilcox's Brigade along with a 12-pounder howitzer from Company A. Because of their shorter range, these seven smoothbore pieces were to target the nearby Federal troops stationed along the Emmitsburg Road. They probably did not move to firing positions on the east side of Pitzer's Woods until McLaws' Division occupied this area.

The battalion's long-range rifled pieces unlimbered along Posey's portion of the line. From this location the five Navy Parrotts, one 3-inch Navy Parrott, Napoleon, and three 10-pounder Parrotts could effectively bombard Cemetery Ridge about 1,400 yards to the east.

Divisional Artillery
Major John Lane
9 Staff and Field Officers

Sumter (Georgia) Artillery - 11th Georgia Battalion

Company A
Captain Hugh M. Ross
1 x 3-inch Navy rifled gun
3 x 10-pounder Parrott rifled guns
1 x 12-pounder howitzer
1 x 12-pounder Napoleon gun
(130 troops present for duty equipped)

Company B
Captain George M. Patterson
4 x 12-pounder howitzers
2 x 12-pounder Napoleon guns
(124 troops present for duty equipped)

Company C
Captain John T. Wingfield
3 x 3-inch Navy rifled guns
2 x 10-pounder Parrott rifled guns
(121 troops present for duty equipped)

III Corps – Heth's Division

Of the four Confederate infantry divisions that fought on July 1, Major-General Henry Heth's Division suffered the most. In Heth's first trial as divisional commander, his unit endured about 40 per cent casualties.

Individual brigades and regiments had taken staggering losses. Davis' Brigade lost about 600 prisoners during its ill-judged plunge into the Railroad Cut. Only two of its nine field officers escaped unhurt. In Pettigrew's Brigade, which suffered about 1,000 casualties, the 26th North Carolina lost more than half its strength including its colonel and lieutenant-colonel. Brigadier-General Archer was captured, leaving the Tennessee Brigade under the command of a lieutenant-colonel. Heth himself was among the wounded and General James Pettigrew, the division's senior yet least experienced brigadier, assumed command.

On July 1, Heth's impetuous but rash leadership had both committed the army prematurely to battle and ruined his division. The division was so battered and shaken that Lee resolved to retain it in reserve for July 2. Accordingly, on the morning of July 2 Anderson's Division relieved Heth's. Heth's men retired from Seminary Ridge to a position about one mile to the rear.

Late on July 1 Brigadier-General James Johnston Pettigrew assumed command of Heth's battered division. During July 2 his men were positioned, as a reserve, well to the rear of III Corps' main deployment. (Carl Smith, Manassas)

HETH'S DIVISION
(not engaged on July 2)
Brigadier-General James Johnston Pettigrew

PETTIGREW'S BRIGADE
Colonel James Keith Marshall
11th Regiment North Carolina Troops
Colonel Collett Leventhorpe
26th Regiment North Carolina Troops
Major John Thomas Jones
47th Regiment North Carolina Troops
Colonel Colonel George H. Faribault
52nd Regiment North Carolina Troops
Lieutenant-Colonel Marcus A. Parks

BROCKENBROUGH'S BRIGADE
Colonel John Mercer Brockenbrough
40th Virginia Infantry Regiment
Captain Thomas Edwin Betts
47th Virginia Infantry Regiment
Colonel Robert Murphy Mayo
55th Virginia Infantry Regiment
Colonel William Steptoe Christian
22nd Battalion Virginia Infantry
Major John Samuel Bowles

ARCHER'S BRIGADE
Lieutenant-Colonel Samuel G. Shephard
13th Alabama Infantry Regiment
Lieutenant-Colonel James Aiken
5th Alabama Infantry Battalion
Major Albert Sebastian Van de Graaff
1st Tennessee Volunteer Infantry Regiment (Provisional Army)
Lieutenant-Colonel Newton J. George
7th Tennessee Infantry Regiment
Colonel John Amenas Fite
14th Tennessee Infantry Regiment
Lieutenant-Colonel James William Lockert

DAVIS' BRIGADE
Brigadier-General Joseph Robert Davis
2nd Mississippi Volunteer Infantry Regiment
Major John Alan Blair
11th Mississippi Volunteer Infantry Regiment
Colonel Francis M. Green
42nd Mississippi Volunteer Infantry Regiment
Colonel Hugh Reid Miller
55th Regiment North Carolina Troops
Captain George Gilreath

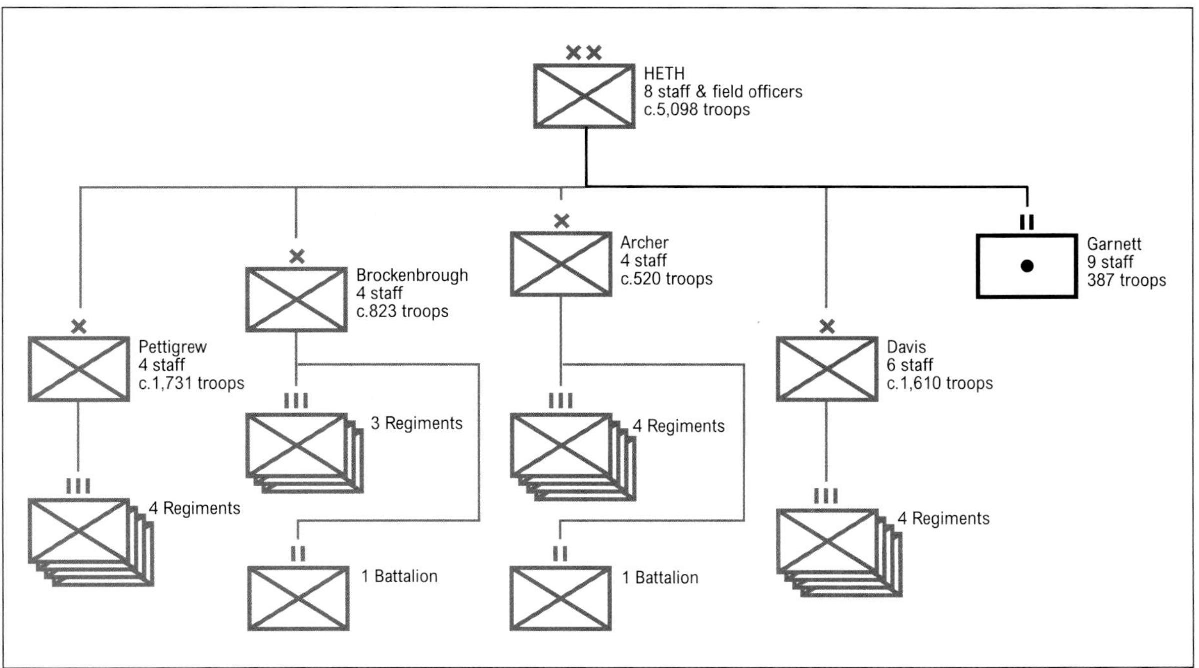

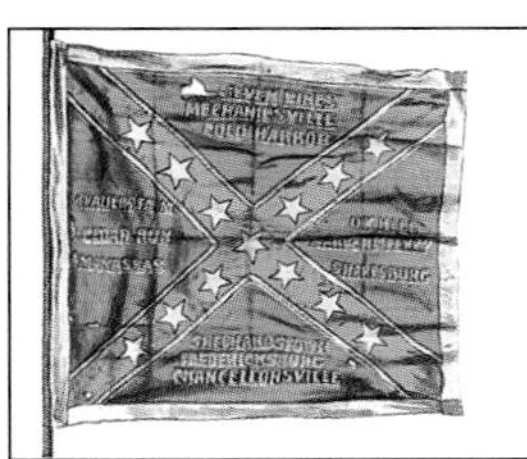

Battle flag of Major Albert Van de Graaff's 1st Tennessee Volunteer Infantry Regiment (Provisional Army).

Battle flag of the 2nd Mississippi Volunteer Infantry Regiment, captured in the battle of the Railroad Cut on July 1.

GARNETT'S BATTALION OF ARTILLERY

Lieutenant-Colonel John Jameson Garnett/ Major Charles Richardson

Donaldsonville Artillery (Louisiana)
Captain Victor Maurin
Huger Battery (Virginia)
Captain Joseph D. Moore
Lewis Artillery (Virginia)
Captain John W. Lewis
Norfolk Light Artillery Blues (Virginia)
Captain Charles R. Grandy

Meanwhile, all of III Corps' artillery was to support Anderson's assault on Cemetery Ridge. Lieutenant-Colonel John Garnett decided that the battalion's smoothbore weapons, two 12-pounder howitzers and four Napoleons, could not be effectively employed. Consequently, on the morning of July 2 he chose to form an all-rifled, nine-gun battery and place it under the control of Major Charles Richardson. Richardson deployed his seven 3-inch rifles and two 10-pounder Parrott rifles on Seminary Ridge to the right of the Hagerstown Road and just south of Schultz's Woods. They were opposite Cemetery Hill. On the left was McIntosh's Battalion while Pegram's Battalion continued the gun line to Richardson's right.

In mid-afternoon Chief of Artillery Colonel Walker had a note delivered to Garnett informing him that Longstreet was soon to attack, and that his guns should assist however they could. At around 1600 hrs Garnett's rifles opened fire and continued until sunset. Because they were in position on Anderson's left, they were the farthest from I Corps' engagement. Their special target was primarily the Union artillery.

Later, when Early's men assaulted Cemetery Hill, the guns again fired on the Federal artillery. 'Just as the sun had disappeared behind the horizon', Garnett reported, 'the enemy's guns were observed to be turned upon a portion of General Ewell's forces.' Richardson's counter-battery fire succeeded, or so Garnett claimed, in diverting the yankee artillery fire from Early's infantry.

III Corps – Pender's Division

Pender's Division passed through Heth's line on July 1 to assault the Federal position on Seminary Ridge. Scales' Brigade was butchered by Union artillery, losing over 500 men and 55 of 56 field officers as well as Scales himself who suffered a severe wound. Perrin's Brigade provided the tactically decisive breakthrough but suffered a loss rate of about 30 per cent. With half the division too battered to fight effectively, Lee decided to keep the division on Seminary Ridge during July 2 where he expected that it would occupy a quiet sector.

On July 2, Pender's Division formed the left of Hill's III Corps. Its front extended from near the Lutheran Seminary south along Seminary Ridge to Anderson's Division. Hill's instructions were to cooperate with Longstreet 'with such of my brigades from the right as could join in with his troops in the attack.' Thus Pender's Division would remain unengaged for the whole day.

Late in the afternoon, Pender rode to the right of his line to see how Longstreet's attack was progressing. Just before sunset a two-inch shell fragment struck

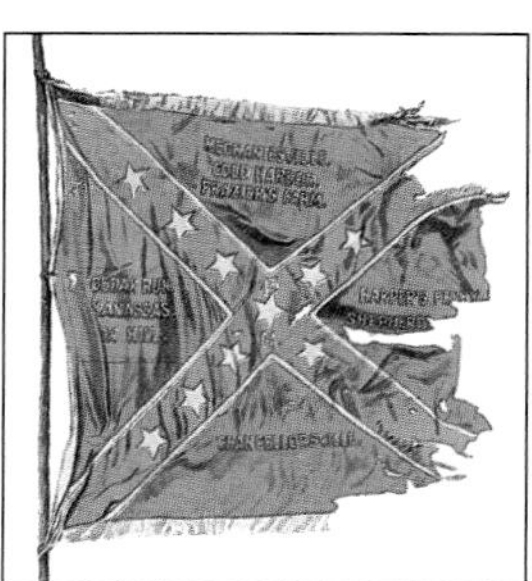

Battle flag of Lieutenant-Colonel Washington Grice's 45th Regiment Georgia Volunteer Infantry.

PENDER'S DIVISION
(deployed but not engaged on July 2)
Major-General William Dorsey Pender/
Brigadier-General James Henry Lane

PERRIN'S BRIGADE
Colonel Abner Monroe Perrin
1st South Carolina Rifles (Orr's Regiment of Rifles)
Captain William M. Hadden
1st South Carolina Regiment (Provisional Army)
Major Comillus Wycliffe McCreary
12th South Carolina Volunteer Regiment
Colonel John Lucas Miller
13th South Carolina Volunteer Regiment
Lieutenant-Colonel Benjamin Thomas Brockman
14th South Carolina Volunteer Regiment
Lieutenant-Colonel Joseph Newton Brown

LANE'S BRIGADE
Brigadier-General James Henry Lane/
Colonel Clark Moulton Avery
7th North Carolina State Troops
Captain J. McLeod Turner
18th Regiment North Carolina Troops
Colonel John Decatur Barry
28th Regiment North Carolina Troops
Colonel Samuel D. Lowe
33rd Regiment North Carolina Troops
Colonel Clark Moulton Avery/
Successor unknown
37th Regiment North Carolina Troops
Colonel William M. Barbour

THOMAS' BRIGADE
Brigadier-General Edward Lloyd Thomas
14th Regiment Georgia Volunteer Infantry
Colonel Robert Warren Folsom
35th Regiment Georgia Volunteer Infantry
Lieutenant-Colonel William Henry McCullohs
45th Regiment Georgia Volunteer Infantry
Lieutenant-Colonel Washington Leonidas Grice
49th Regiment Georgia Volunteer Infantry
Colonel Samuel Thomas Player

SCALES' BRIGADE
Colonel William Lee Joshua Lowrance
13th Regiment North Carolina Troops
Lieutenant Robert L. Moir
16th Regiment North Carolina Troops
Captain Leroy W. Stowe
22nd Regiment North Carolina Troops
Colonel James Conner
34th Regiment North Carolina Troops
Lieutenant-Colonel George T. Gordon
38th Regiment North Carolina Troops
Lieutenant John M. Robinson

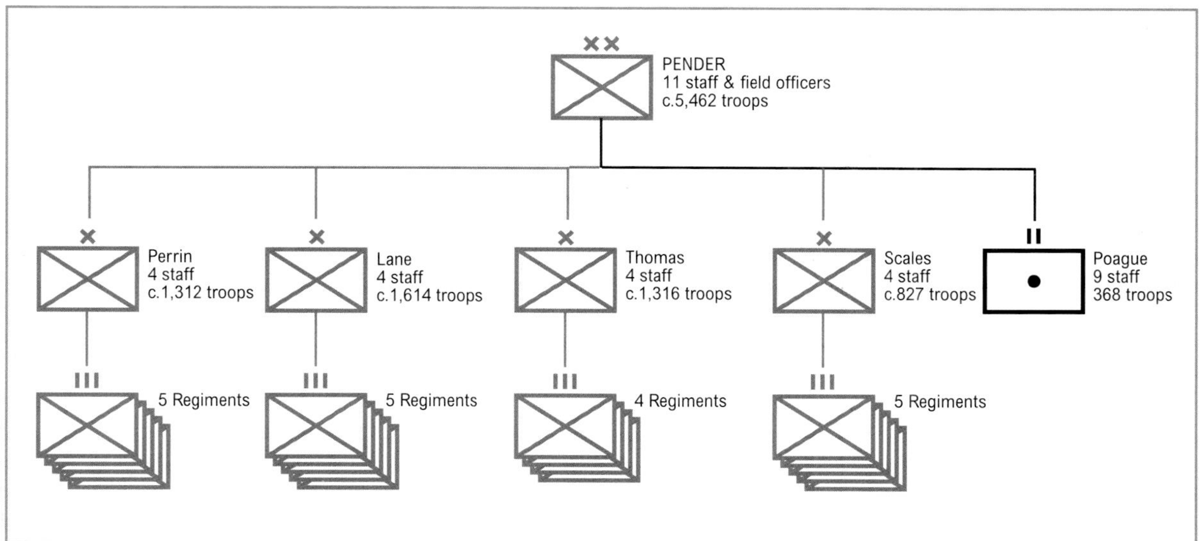

Major-General William Dorsey Pender received the order to attack late on July 1. The young officer had been promoted to divisional command barely a month earlier and performed superbly at Seminary Ridge. He was to receive a mortal wound on July 2.
(Carl Smith, Manassas)

him in the thigh. Pender did not think the wound serious but had to yield command to Brigadier-General Lane. In the event, the wound proved fatal.

Ewell informed Lane that he would advance on Cemetery Hill at dark. Lane ordered Brigadier-General Thomas' and Colonel Perrin's Brigades to advance to protect the right flank of Rodes' Division. Lane supported these two brigades with his own brigade, now commanded by Colonel Avery, and with Scales' Brigade, now commanded by Colonel Lowrance who had reported for duty although he had been wounded the previous day. When Rodes declined to charge,

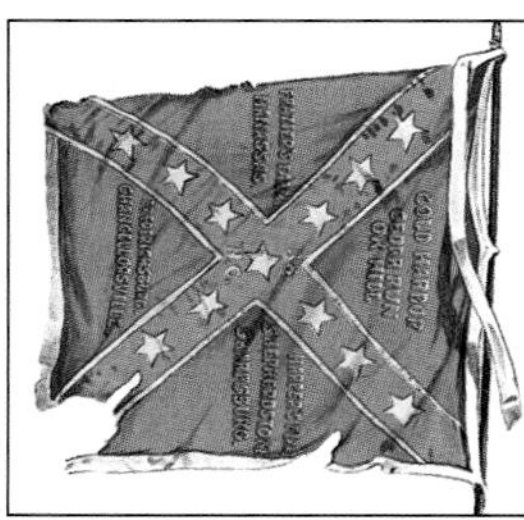

Battle flag of the 38th Regiment North Carolina Troops.

Thomas and Perrin remained in their advanced position. Except for the loss of Pender, the division suffered negligible casualties on July 2.

Major William Poague's artillery battalion had departed Cashtown to move to Gettysburg at 1100 hrs on July 1. The battalion comprised four, four-gun batteries representing three different states. It did not participate in the day's battle.

The battalion remained in reserve until late in the afternoon of July 2 when Poague received an order from Walker to report to Major-General Anderson. The re-deployment was apparently difficult. Poague writes that he 'at last succeeded in getting ten of my guns into position. The balance (six howitzers) were kept a short distance in rear, as no place could be found from which they could be used with advantage.'

The three rifles and two Napoleons were posted on Anderson's left. Five more Napoleons unlimbered to these guns' right some four hundred yards farther south along the ridge. Poague estimated the range to Cemetery Ridge as 1,400 yards. His guns apparently did not fire on July 2.

POAGUE'S BATTALION OF ARTILLERY
Major William Thomas Poague

Madison Light Artillery (Mississippi)
Captain George Ward
Albemarle Artillery (Virginia)
Captain James Walter Wyatt
Co.C. 10th North Carolina State Troops
Captain Joseph Graham
Brooke's Battery (Virginia)
Lieutenant Addison W. Utterback

III Corps' Reserve Artillery

Major William Pegram's battalion had the unusual composition of five batteries. It had the army's most modern weaponry with four 10-pounder Parrotts, four 3-inch rifles, ten Napoleons, and two Whitworth 3-inch rifles.

The battalion unlimbered on Seminary Ridge in front of McMillan's Woods. From left to right the order was: the Letcher Artillery, the Purcell Artillery, the Pee Dee Artillery, the Crenshaw Battery and the Fredericksburg Artillery. The battalion's official report relates that its guns 'opened upon the enemy at intervals, enfilading their batteries whenever they opened upon the batteries on our right.'

Three of the four batteries commanded by Major McIntosh delivered supporting fire on July 2. Hurt's Hardaway Artillery deployed in Schultz's Woods just south of the Hagerstown Road. Johnson's Virginia Battery and the Second Rockbridge Artillery were on Hurt's right. Rice's battery remained in reserve.

McIntosh's Battalion possessed the army's two Whitworth rifles. The English-manufactured Whitworth was a breech-loading rifled gun that combined accuracy and superior penetration with a five-mile range. During the artillery duel on July 2, one 3-inch rifle was hit on its muzzle and disabled while the axle on one of the Whitworths broke, forcing its retirement for repairs.

III Army Corps Reserve Artillery
Colonel Reuben Lindsay Walker
4 Staff and Field Officers

Pegram's Battalion of Artillery
Major William Johnson Pegram

Pee Dee Artillery (South Carolina)
Lieutenant William E. Zimmerman
4 x 3-inch rifled guns
(65 troops present for duty equipped)

Crenshaw Battery (Virginia)
Lieutenant Andrew B. Johnston
2 x 12-pounder Napoleon guns
2 x 12-pounder howitzers
(76 troops present for duty equipped)

Fredericksburg Artillery (Virginia)
Captain Edward Avenmore Marye
2 x 3-inch rifled guns
2 x 12-pounder Napoleon guns
(71 troops present for duty equipped)

Letcher Artillery (Virginia)
Captain Thomas Alexander Brander
2 x 10-pounder Parrott rifled guns
2 x 12-pounder Napoleon guns
(65 troops present for duty equipped)

Purcell Artillery (Virginia)
Captain Joseph McGraw
4 x 12-pounder Napoleon guns
(89 troops present for duty equipped)

McIntosh's Battalion of Artillery
Major David Gregg McIntosh

Hardaway Artillery (Alabama)
Captain William B. Hurt
2 x 3-inch rifled guns
2 x Whitworth guns
(71 troops present for duty equipped)

Danville Artillery (Virginia)
Captain Robert Sidney Rice
4 x 12-pounder Napoleon Guns
(114 troops present for duty equipped)

2nd Rockbridge Artillery (Virginia)
Lieutenant Samuel Wallace
2 x 3-inch rifled guns
2 x 12-pounder Napoleon guns
(67 troops present for duty equipped)

Jackson's Flying Artillery (Virginia)
Captain Marmaduke Johnson
4 x 3-inch rifled guns
(96 troops present for duty equipped)

ARMY OF NORTHERN VIRGINIA III CORPS' BATTLES

Anderson's Division

Anderson Goes In – 1800–1930 hrs

On July 2 Major-General Richard Anderson's Division received orders to occupy a position on Pender's right along Seminary Ridge. The evening before, Brigadier-General Wilcox had been posted on the division's right near the Black Horse Tavern. While taking up its new position on Seminary Ridge shortly before noon on July 2, Wilcox's skirmishers encountered a yankee reconnaissance in force. The combat occurred on the border of Pitzer's Woods. Green-clad Federal sharpshooters fired at the 11th Alabama, dropping its major and driving back its skirmish line. When the sharpshooters pursued into the open, the 10th Alabama delivered a telling volley. Supported by the 8th Alabama, the 10th pressed the enemy hard. Wilcox reported that the fight lasted only 20 minutes before the enemy ceded the ground. The 10th Alabama lost 10 killed and 28 wounded while the 11th suffered 18 wounded.

Thereafter, Anderson's five-brigade line stretched for a mile along the wooded, forward slope of Seminary Ridge. The enemy line on Cemetery Ridge was in plain view with the nearest battle line only 800 yards to the east. Three III Corps artillery battalions belonging to Pegram, McIntosh, and Lane as well as the nine rifled pieces in Garnett's Battalion provided fire support. In addition, after McLaws' Division cleared the Peach Orchard, Colonel Porter Alexander ordered his artillery battalion to advance to the recently captured high ground. Here they found numerous splendid targets among the nearby defeated enemy units. But Alexander could, for the first time, see that there was another enemy position that had to be conquered. It 'loomed up near 1,000 yards beyond us, a ridge giving good cover behind it & endless fine positions for batteries.' Alexander observed rallied Union troops joining with fresh formations to occupy these positions along Cemetery Ridge. This would be the objective for Anderson's Division.

Anderson's Division had deployed under the eyes of both corps commander A.P. Hill and General Lee. Hill informed Anderson that he was to advance his brigades as soon as Longstreet's attack reached his front. The charge was to be made sequentially by brigade from right to left.

Yet otherwise, communication among senior leaders was poor. Wilcox's Brigade, on Anderson's left, failed to occupy a satisfactory start line before the division advanced. At 1700 hrs, all that Colonel David Lang of the Florida Brigade knew was that with Longstreet engaged, he 'was to advance with General Wilcox, holding all the ground the enemy yielded.'

Wilcox's four regiments formed east of Spangler's Woods to begin an uphill march toward the Emmitsburg Road. Perry's small Florida Brigade dutifully conformed to this advance. Both brigades advanced through a deadly artillery fire from Union batteries along the Emmitsburg Road. Fortunately for them, Barksdale's Brigade, having just broken through the Peach Orchard, was advancing northeast along the road to take the Federal gun line in flank.

The Confederates were disordered by the difficult advance. Rather than halt to dress ranks, they pressed forward to capitalise upon their enemy's distress. Wilcox's and Perry's brigades chased the yankees to the base of Cemetery Ridge. Here they halted to reform. Their commanders urgently sent messages to Anderson asking for reinforcements.

Brigadier-General Ambrose Wright's Brigade occupied a position on Seminary Ridge just to the left of Perry's Brigade. Wright deployed three regiments in his main battle line. The 2nd Georgia Battalion deployed as skirmishers to cover the brigade front. Wright intended for this battalion to form on the brigade's left once the advance began. Wright's orders

1200 hrs	1300	1400	1500	1600	1700	1800	1900	2000	2100	2200
pages 30-31				32-39,67-69	40-43			70-73		

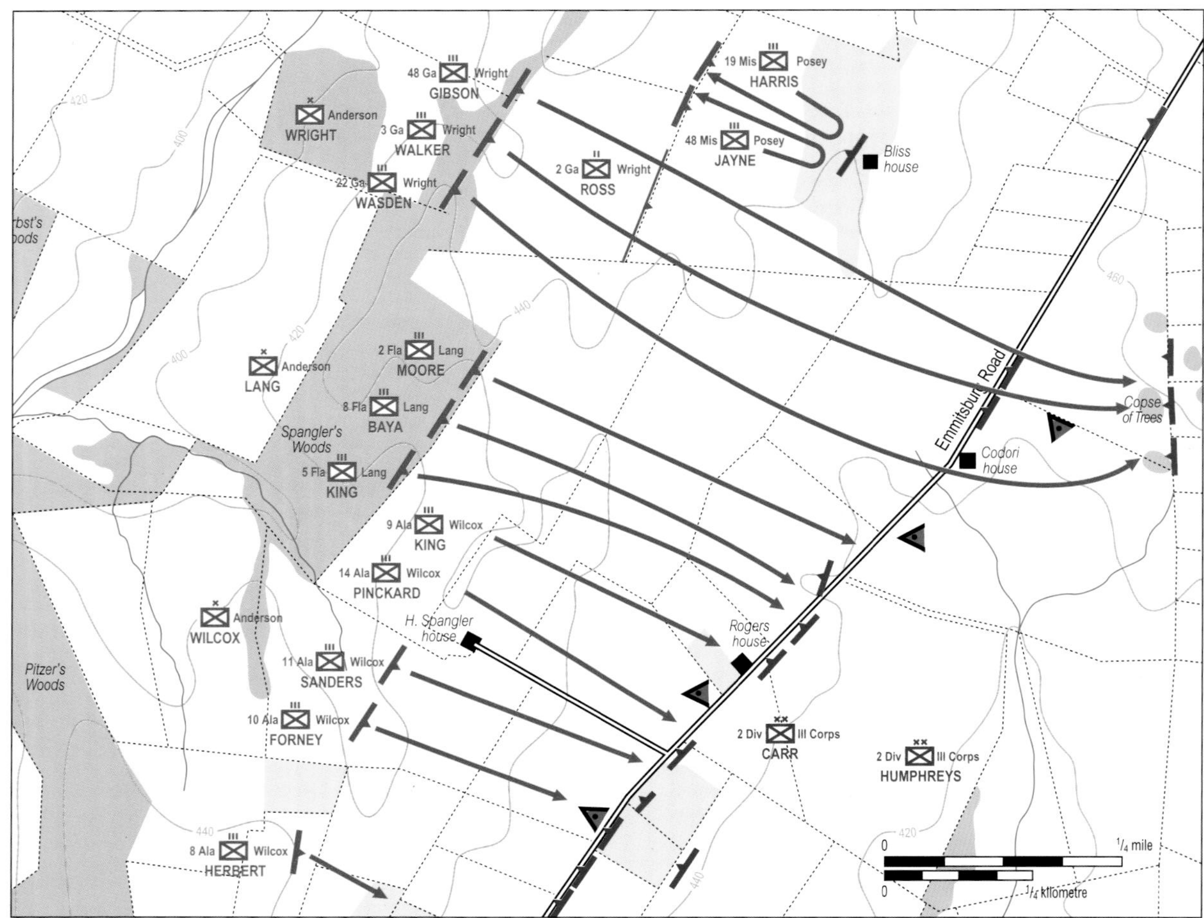

Anderson's Division achieved initial success in its assault towards the Emmitsburg Road. However lack of support and superior Union strength forced it to relinquish its grasp of Cemetery Ridge.

were to move forward when Perry advanced. He expected that Posey's Brigade, on his left, would advance at the same time. Indeed, these were Posey's orders.

About 500 yards in front of Anderson's position on Seminary Ridge stood the Bliss Farm. At a fence line midway to the farm, Posey had deployed elements of his 16th and 19th Mississippi Regiments as skirmishers. Some time before Wright advanced, a staff officer arrived from Anderson and instructed Posey to move forward with two regiments in skirmish formation. Apparently Anderson wanted the Bliss Farm cleared before the main effort began. Posey sent the balance of the 19th Mississippi as well as the 48th Mississippi.

A reinforced Union regiment held the Bliss Farm. It served as the anchor for the Federal skirmish line. A fierce outpost skirmish ensued. Initially Posey's men prevailed. However, a yankee counter-attack reclaimed the position. According to one Union officer, his men captured 92 men and 7 officers in the Bliss barn.

When Wright began his advance, Federal forces still controlled the Bliss Farm. Wright's Brigade began its advance about the same time as Perry's Florida Brigade. When it reached the fence where stood the 2nd Georgia Battalion, Wright's plan miscarried. Instead of forming in mass on the brigade's left, the skirmishers simply merged with the main battle line. Thus, when the brigade charged, its left flank was unsecured. If, however, Posey conformed to Wright's advance, this error would not be too significant.

Wright's Brigade paused to gather breath in a

1200 hrs	1300	1400	1500	1600	1700	1800	1900	2000	2100	2200
pages 30-31				32-39,67-69	40-43			70-73		

depression in the ground and then advanced towards the Codori House. It confronted two defending regiments supported by two batteries along the Emmitsburg Road. As Wright pressed ahead, he realised that Posey was not advancing. He sent a staff officer to complain to Major-General Anderson. The reply came that Posey had been ordered forward, that Anderson would repeat the order, and meanwhile, carry on.

Because of the Union resistance at the Bliss Farm, Posey had added the remainder of his 16th Mississippi to the fight for the farm. When they were not enough, he personally led the 12th Mississippi into the fray. At the same time, Posey requested support from Brigadier-General William Mahone's Brigade. Thus, at the time Wright perceived that he was unsupported, Posey's entire brigade was embroiled in a contest with the Union skirmish line.

Slowly, Posey's men pushed forward towards the Emmitsburg Road. However, their advance lagged behind Wright's Brigade. At this point, although no one on the scene understood it, Anderson's Division was in disarray. Its three right-hand brigades – Wilcox, Perry, Wright – had charged as intended. They stood on the brink of success. Each brigade commander had requested reinforcements. Wilcox recalled that he asked three separate times. Although Mahone's Brigade remained available, no support arrived. Meanwhile, Posey had squandered his brigade by piecemeal commitment.

Wright's men had a brief fight against the ineptly-stationed Union line along the Emmitsburg Road. Passing along both sides of the Codori buildings, the Georgians ascended the slope of Cemetery Ridge. They marched straight for a large gap in the Federal line. However, from just past the copse of trees, two Union batteries blasted them with canister. Musketry from the yankee infantry behind a low, stone wall flailed Wright's left flank. Shrugging off their losses, the Georgians reached the crestline. They had pierced the Union centre but stood vulnerable unless reinforcements arrived very soon.

Help was not forthcoming. Instead came a series of Federal counter-attacks. A fresh brigade struck Barksdale's Brigade and drove it from his position along Plum Run. Its retreat uncovered Wilcox's right flank. The 1st Minnesota charged valiantly directly at Wilcox. A Federal battery stationed about 300 yards away pelted the brigade with canister. With no support in view and both flanks threatened, Wilcox ordered a retreat back to the Emmitsburg Road. Then and thereafter, Wilcox believed that had there been a supporting line, his brigade would have carried the heights. His brigade suffered 577 casualties on July 2.

Meanwhile, the Florida Brigade had driven all before it, in spite of 'a murderous fire of grape, canister, and musketry.' It charged at the double until it encountered a mix of rallied enemy units on Cemetery Ridge. As Colonel Lang tried to reform his lines, Union troops appeared only 50 yards away and opened a heavy fire from the crest of the ridge. Nearly simultaneously, an aide reported that a heavy hostile force was advancing against the adjacent brigade commanded by Wilcox. Seeing Wilcox withdraw, Lang also ordered a retreat. The gallant Floridians, having lost about 300 of the 700 men who began the advance, retired to Spangler's Woods.

It appeared to General Wright that his brigade stood alone. He complained in his official report that when his brigade gained the crest of Cemetery Ridge, the Florida Brigade was retiring and Posey had failed to advance. No one was ever able to account satisfactorily for why Posey mishandled his brigade and why Mahone never entered the fray. Posey's Brigade suffered only 83 casualties this day.

In Wright's words, 'We were now within less than 100 yards of the heights, which were lined with artillery, supported by a strong body of infantry, under protection of a stone fence.' Still the brigade struggled forward with its right wing actually gaining the crest. In all likelihood Wright's men pushed farther east than did any of the Confederate soldiers involved in Pickett's charge the next day. An overwhelming collection of rallied and fresh Union soldiers counter-attacked. Isolated and outnumbered, Wright's men yielded. A short yankee pursuit captured a number of Georgians around the Codori House. Wright's Brigade lost 688 men during its gallant charge.

Wright's retreat marked the end of the great Confederate effort to envelop the Union left and pierce its centre. Eleven Confederate brigades had fought and bettered some 22 Union brigades. Like Long-street's troops, Anderson's three brigades that had carried the brunt of the effort suffered severe losses. About 1,600 men, or 40 per cent of the men involved in the brigades of Wilcox, Perry and Wright were casualties. Wilcox and Wright each lost three out of four regimental commanders.

Stuart's Cavalry Division

After an exhausting overnight ride, Stuart's cavalry entered Dover on the morning of July 1. They had no idea that they had crossed the path of Early's march towards Gettysburg. Worse, Stuart still had no idea where Lee and the army lay. Stuart gave his troopers a badly-needed four-hour rest. Then the column set out for Carlisle. It had to cross the northernmost spur of South Mountain, an exercise that badly depleted the already very tired men and horses. By the time the column approached Carlisle, it had covered nearly 40 miles since morning. An officer reported that 'the men were overcome and so tired and stupid as almost to be ignorant of what was taking place around them.'

Instead of finding Confederate infantry belonging to Ewell's Corps, the cavalry encountered enemy infantry in Carlisle. The horse artillery tried to drive them out with a desultory shelling that continued until near midnight. Finally, at 0100 hrs on July 2 Stuart obtained orders that informed him that the Army of Northern Virginia was at Gettysburg where it had been engaged since morning. Lee ordered Stuart to hurry to rejoin his command by way of Heidlersburg and Hunterstown. By 0200 hrs the column was under way again.

CAVALRY DIVISION
Major-General James Ewell Brown Stuart

HAMPTON'S BRIGADE
Colonel Laurence Simmons Baker
9th North Carolina State Troops (1st Cavalry)
Lieutenant-Colonel James B. Gordon
1st South Carolina Regiment of Cavalry
Colonel John Logan Black
2nd South Carolina Regiment of Cavalry
Colonel Mathew Calbraith Butler
Cobb's (Georgia) Legion Cavalry
Colonel Pierce B.M. Young
Jefferson Davis Legion (Mississippi)
Colonel Joseph Frederick Waring
Phillips' (Georgia) Legion Cavalry
Lieutenant-Colonel William W. Rich

Between noon and 1400 hrs the column passed through Hunterstown, which was picketed by a detached squadron of the Cobb Legion. When Federal cavalry pressed this squadron, a skirmish ensued in which Brigadier-General Wade Hampton received a grazing gunshot wound and a sabre cut. Hampton

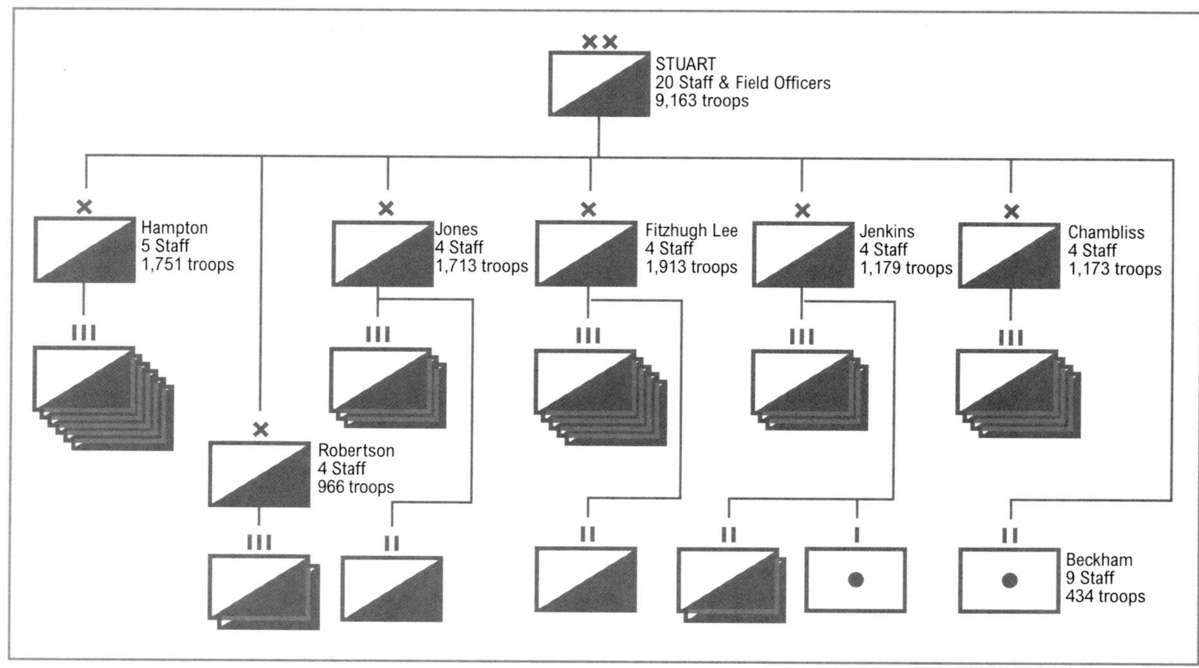

CAVALRY DIVISION (continued)

ROBERTSON'S BRIGADE
(not engaged at Gettysburg)
Brigadier-General Beverly Holcombe Robertson
59th Regiment North Carolina Troops (4th Cavalry)
Colonel Dennis Dozier Ferebee
63rd Regiment North Carolina Troops (5th Cavalry)
Colonel Peter G. Evans

JONES' BRIGADE
(not engaged at Gettysburg)
Brigadier-General William Edmonson Jones
6th Regiment Virginia Cavalry
Major Cabell Edward Flournoy
7th Regiment Virginia Cavalry
Colonel Thomas A. Marshall, Jr.
11th Regiment Virginia Cavalry
Colonel Lunsford Lindsay Lomax

FITZHUGH LEE'S BRIGADE
Brigadier-General Fitzhugh Lee
1st Maryland Cavalry Battalion
Major Harry Gilmor
1st Regiment Virginia Cavalry
Colonel James Henry Drake
2nd Regiment Virginia Cavalry
Colonel Thomas Taylor Munford
3rd Regiment Virginia Cavalry
Colonel Thomas Howerton Owen
4th Regiment Virginia Cavalry
Colonel William Carter Wickham
5th Regiment Virginia Cavalry
Colonel Thomas Lafayette Rosser

JENKINS' BRIGADE
Brigadier-General Albert Gallatin Jenkins/
Colonel James Cochran
14th Regiment Virginia Cavalry
Colonel James Cochran/
Major Benjamin Eakle
16th Regiment Virginia Cavalry
Colonel Milton J. Ferguson
17th Regiment Virginia Cavalry
Colonel William Henderson French
34th Battalion Virginia Cavalry
Lieutenant-Colonel Vincent Addison Witcher
36th Battalion Virginia Cavalry
Colonel Charles Edmonson Thorburn
Kanawha Horse Artillery (Virginia)
Captain Thomas E. Jackson

WILLIAM HENRY FITZHUGH LEE'S BRIGADE
Colonel John Randolph Chambliss, Jr.
19th North Carolina State Troops (2nd Cavalry)
Lieutenant-Colonel William H.F. Payne
9th Regiment Virginia Cavalry
Colonel Richard Lee Turberville Beale
10th Regiment Virginia Cavalry
Colonel James Lucius Davis
13th Regiment Virginia Cavalry
Lieutenant-Colonel Jefferson Curle Phillips

BECKHAM'S BATTALION OF ARTILLERY
Major Robert Franklin Beckham

1st Stuart Horse Artillery (Virginia)
Captain James Breathed
Ashby Artillery (Virginia)
Captain Roger Preston Chew
2nd Maryland Artillery (Baltimore Light)
Captain William H. Griffin
Washington Artillery (South Carolina)
Captain James Franklin Hart
2nd Stuart Horse Artillery (Virginia)
Captain William Morrell McGregor
Beauregard Rifles - Stuart Horse Artillery (Virginia)
Captain Marcellus Newton Moorman

refused to relinquish command. Two hours later, Hampton led his brigade back to Hunterstown to assist the Cobb Legion. Here they easily repelled a foolish charge delivered by Custer's cavalry.

Meanwhile, the brigades commanded by Fitz Lee and Chambliss had proceeded towards Gettysburg. Stuart rode ahead to report to Lee at his headquarters a mile west of Gettysburg. Coldly Lee inquired, 'General Stuart, where have you been?'

Taken aback, Stuart tried to explain. Lee angrily interrupted: 'I have not heard a word from you for days, and you the eyes and ears of my army!'

Embarrassed staff officers averted their eyes and one later recalled that Stuart looked like a man who had just taken a blow to the face. In his official report, Lee implied that Stuart's march towards Gettysburg was overly slow and that the army's operations were 'much embarrassed by the absence of the cavalry.'

IMBODEN'S COMMAND
(guarding baggage - not engaged at Gettysburg)
Brigadier-General John Daniel Imboden

18th Regiment Virginia Cavalry
Colonel George William Imboden
914 troops
62nd Regiment Virginia Mounted Infantry
Colonel George Hugh Smith
1,095 troops
Virginia Partisan Rangers
Captain John Hanson McNeill
90 troops
McClanahan's Battery
Captain John H. McClanahan
142 troops

WARGAMING GETTYSBURG – July 2

As noted in the earlier volumes, to fight a well-known battle such as Gettysburg with historical miniatures on a tabletop presents a considerable challenge. Students of the battle recognise the grand tactical errors that the rival commanders committed and are unlikely to repeat them.

If given free play, a Confederate player will probably put in every man to capture Little Round Top, a position perceived only after the battle as the field's key terrain. Unlike his historical counterparts, he will bypass opposition where necessary and speed to capture this vital high ground. On the other hand, if the player is constrained in a historical manner, a re-fight of July 2 does offer the compelling drama of trying to change the history of one of the war's pivotal engagements.

A gamer has two choices: deploy the forces in their historical positions as of 1600 hrs on July 2; or wargame a series of historical, and intense tactical challenges built around the day's key encounters.

If opting for the former, it makes sense to concentrate on Longstreet's abortive flank attack. We can eliminate Cemetery Hill and Culp's Hill and the opposing forces on these sectors. As we have seen, without an overwhelming Union blunder (which admittedly almost occurred when XII Corps denuded Culp's Hill) these hills could not be successfully attacked.

Begin the action with a Confederate artillery bombardment. Then Longstreet's infantry start their *en echelon* assault. Initially, the rebel brigades should be required to advance against the nearest enemy, as they actually performed. Supposing they break the crust of the Union line, the gamer can roll an initiative die to determine if the successful brigade must continue along the axis of its charge or whether it can manoeuvre optimally to take advantage of its breakthrough. As we have seen, Benning's Brigade 'failed' its initiative roll and continued to hammer away at the Devil's Den whereas Barksdale's Brigade made its breakthrough and then wheeled to roll up the defenders' line in the Peach Orchard.

The Longstreet game is best played by adhering to the historical timing of the Confederate advance, but to replicate some 'fog of war', the Union player should not know that the rebels are being historically constrained. Alternatively, a simple table can be built to govern the release of the Confederate brigades and to duplicate the uneasy timing of their *en echelon* attack.

Re-fighting the Longstreet attack should create an exciting, swirling battle as the series of rebel assaults explode against the Union line. Alternatively, if the gamer wants to fight on a more tactical level, July 2 is full of opportunity. Clearly the contest for Little Round Top is among the most attractive challenges, but the encounters in the Wheatfield, the defence of Stony Hill, the struggle for the Bliss Farm or even a night action built around Early's attack against Cemetery Hill can offer excellent games.

SELECT BIBLIOGRAPHY

Busey, John W. and Martin, David G. *Regimental Strengths and Losses at Gettysburg.* Highstown: Longstreet House, 1982.

Coddington, Edwin B. *The Gettysburg Campaign: A study in Command.* New York: Charles Scribner's Sons, 1968.

Fox, William F. *Regimental Losses in the American Civil War, 1861-1865.* Albany: Albany Publishing Co., 1898.

Luvas, Jay and Harold W. Nelson, eds. *The U.S. Army War College Guide to the Battle of Gettysburg.* Carlisle, PA: South Mountain Press, 1986.

Pfanz, Harry W. *Gettysburg: Culp's Hill and Cemetery Hill.* Chapel Hill: University of North Carolina Press, 1993.

Pfanz, Harry W. *Gettysburg: The Second Day.* Chapel Hill: University of North Carolina Press, 1987.

Tagg, Larry. *The Generals of Gettysburg.* Campbell, CA: Savas Publishing, 1998.

U.S. War Department. *War of the Rebellion: A Compilation of the Official Records of the Union and Confederate Armies.* Series I, vol. 27. Washington: Government Printing Office, 1889.

Wise, Jennings Cropper. *The Long Arm of Lee.* 2 vols. Lynchburg, VA: J.P. Bell Co., 1915.